Government
Marketing
Best
Practices

Government Marketing Best Practices

Real World Tactics on
How to Grow Mindshare
and Increase Marketshare
to Grab a Bigger Slice
of the World's Largest Market
– "Fortune One" –
the U.S. Federal Government

by
Mark Amtower

GOVERNMENT MARKET PRESS

Published by Government Market Press
P.O. Box 314
Highland, MD 20777

Printed by Bookmasters
2541 Ashland Rd.
Mansfield, OH 44905

Design by Rome Graphics Design
www.romegraphics.com

Library of Congress Control Number: 2004195116

Amtower, Mark, 1950 -
Government Marketing Best Practices : Real world tactics on
how to grow mindshare and increase marketshare to grab a bigger slice of the
world's largest market—fortune one—the U.S. Federal Government /
Mark Amtower.

ISBN 0-9764-8670-9

Advance Praise for
Government Marketing Best Practices

*In this book, Mark follows his usual no-nonsense approach, getting
right to the heart of what to do and not do when it comes to selling to
the government. Whether you think having the Federal Government as a
customer is simple or complicated, Mark sets the record straight.
For those who want to know how to really do business with the government,
this book should be required reading.*
**Calvin L. Hackeman, Managing Partner, Technology Industry
Practice, Grant Thornton LLP**

*Mark Amtower is the Dean of Government Marketing! He must find it
incredibly frustrating to watch many of us make mistakes as we slowly learn
what he already knows. When Mark Amtower speaks, I listen very carefully!*
Dendy Young, CEO, GTSI Corp.

*Mark Amtower is without a doubt the leading authority on B2G marketing.
This book is the essence of what he has been talking about for 20 years.*
**Bob Bly, author of Business to Business Direct Marketing & world
renowned copywriter**

*Buy this book . . . Do everything Mark Amtower says . . . Go to the
bank! If you are selling to the government — or want to — this is the Bible
of government marketing and you need it! Nobody knows more about
successful marketing to the government market than Mark Amtower.*
**Don Libey, Libey Incorporated, Advisors and Investment Bankers
to the Direct Marketing Industry**

My experience with Mark Amtower has been very enlightening, to say the least. It's kind of like fishing in the Florida Everglades—you might catch a fish on your own, but you can also get eaten by an alligator—you're better off with an experienced guide. I've heard Mark speak on at least 15 separate occasions and I learn something new each time. He tells it to you like it is—a rare trait in Washington—"not that he has an opinion." I want every one of my clients to read this book!
David Powell, Vice President and COO, Federal Business Council

Nobody gets down in the trenches of Federal marketing like Mark Amtower and his new book, Government Marketing Best Practices, is full of great ideas, well proven tactics and the basic fundamentals of Federal marketing, necessary to successfully drive your government sales. His comprehensive, direct and sometimes off-beat view of what it takes to be successful in the Federal space, is backed up by decades of being on the front lines, rolling around in the trenches and back alleys of the government's unique acquisition modes and procurement preferences. Government Marketing Best Practices is a book that should be read by both Federal contractor wannabes and those that have been flailing away at it for years with mixed results. Even market leaders in the government space will find this book useful for rejuvenating tired or off-the-mark marketing campaigns to help regain lost mindshare and beat back the competition. The road to success in the Federal space is littered with good products and services that made it the commercial world, but did not translate well in the government market. Amtower's tactical and practical approach will help you define your true space within the Federal enterprise and ultimately net the results you deserve.
Mark Meudt, Marketing Executive Director for Alcatel Government Solutions

Mark Amtower is well known for his expertise in government marketing and ready opinions on every subject known to man. This book is no holds barred.
Alan Bechara, PC Mall-Gov

Mark Amtower practically invented the B2G market for catalogers. Government Marketing Best Practices reveals the secrets of the trade that have helped his clients build significant government business.
George Mosher, President, National Business Furniture

The chapter on Direct Mail was particularly useful and chock-full of practical tips for marketers
who need to get high response rates from promos to the Feds.
Anne Holland, Publisher, Marketing Sherpa

Table of Contents

Acknowledgements

This market — any market — is about relationships. Careers are about who you know, when you know them, and what people think about you. If people like you and respect what you do, they will be in positions to help you in various ways, and they will be inclined to do just that. Conversely, people who know you and don't like you will be in positions to stifle you and your career at some point.

Over the past 20 years I have been fortunate in many ways, not the least of which is the friendships I have developed in the markets in which I ply my trade. I will not try to list all of those who have been important in my growth, as there have been too many and I would inadvertently leave many deserving names off the list.

There are four sets of people I need to recognize: those who inhabit the "inside the Beltway" world of the Federal market, those in the direct marketing arena, the clients who overlap these respective markets who have helped me grow, and the editors and reporters who have spent time with me over the years.

If I had a mentor in the government market, it was Lynn Bateman, who through the 1970s and 1980s was the advisor to many integrators and resellers on matters involving contractual nuances. Lynn and I developed a friendship that continues today, even though she has long since left the market. She convinced me early on to trust my instincts, and by example, showed me that being me was the best way to go. She would constantly tell me to say what I thought, that my instincts were good.

Dendy Young, then of Falcon Microsystems and currently the CEO of GSTI, was the first senior executive to meet with me regularly. Although no longer a client, he is certainly a friend.

Lynn and Dendy would remind me right here to say that I couldn't do any of this without the invaluable assistance of my wife and business partner, Mary Ellen. Mary Ellen runs the "business" side of our business, which frees me to write, speak and otherwise irritate the world at large.

Lisa Dezzutti of Market Connections was once an occasional client (when she was with GTSI) and is still a friend, but also a valuable resource as her company does the best research in this market. You will see it throughout this book.

Judy Bradt of Summit Insight gave me my first speaking engagement when she was the Commercial Officer for the Canadian Embassy in the late 1980s. I must say I was, um, pretty, er, bad back then. But they loved what I had to say. Since then many, including David Powell of the Federal Business Council and Chuck Tannen (former owner of the Direct Marketing to Business conference) have invited me to speak at events all over the country. I am somewhat better now than I was then.

There are others that need to be mentioned. John Sanders, who was the publisher of Washington Technology, in the early days, is still a good friend and occasional advisor. Al Vingelis of NCS Direct, who has managed data for me for over twenty years, is the only person I trust with my data. Tom Hewitt, founder of Federal Sources, met with me regularly throughout the 1990s. Dan Young is one of the true gentlemen in the market, formerly with Federal Data Corporation and on the Board of many companies. Jerry McFaul of the U.S. Geological Survey remains one of the most enthusiastic Federal employees I've ever had the pleasure to work with. Bob Greeves is now with DOJ as a result of a conversation we had when he was considering retiring. I did some consulting with Bob when he was with the National Academy of Public Administration, where I was on an advisory board with the talented Olga Grkavac of ITAA. Bob Harar is the founder of FOSE, and put me on my first official Board of Advisors. Fern Krauss is the government public relations professional who also edits my stuff to make me look semi-literate.

In the direct marketing/e-marketing world there are also many, including my personal advisors: Amy Africa, Joanna Brandi, Bob Bly, Michael Brown, Ralph Drybrough, Victor Hunter, Don (the real "Donald") Libey, Mac McIntosh, Neil Sexton, Debbie Weil and others.

On the client side, lots of people have funded my education, allowing us to learn together what works for them. David Collins of Learning Tree International, Scott Heller of National Audio Visual, George Mosher of National Business Furniture, Jim Shanks of CDW-G, are among the hundred or so that should be listed.

The business press, both the government trade press and the marketing trade press, have been generous in their coverage of me, my career and my niche. Anne Armstrong, Chris Dorobek and the staff of Federal Computer Week, Tad Clark and Glenn Kalinoski of DM News, Mark Del Franco and everyone at Catalog Age, Carol Krol of BtoB, Larry Riggs and Ray Schultz of Direct magazine, Tom Temin and the crew at Government Computer News, the editors of the now-defunct Reseller Management and Marketing Computers and many more.

There are many others, who will simply have to accept my gratitude.

Please keep this in mind as you read this book: these *relationships* have all helped me not only grow my business and my network, they have helped me to grow. Many of the people I have worked with in the last 20 years are still friends, and they remain important to me personally and professionally. This is a market where relationships truly count. My career would be negligible without the relationships I have developed and maintained over the years.

To each I owe a tremendous debt.

Introduction

Myths from the Federal Market

Over the past few years, there has been a renewed interest in selling to the Federal government. In large part this is because of the slowdown in the rest of the economy, fallout from 9-11, and the fact that government spends billions each year. The U.S. government market—federal, state and local—represents **25% of the Gross National Product** and **20 million employees**. Furthermore, governments buy every legitimate business product and service imaginable, from information technology to furniture to toilet paper.

While the interest in the Federal market continues to grow, the market perceptions are, at best, blurred to most. From Wall Street to Silicon Valley, the amount of misinformation and half-truths about this market abound, always on the periphery of otherwise intelligent business meetings.

Part of this perception is because we in the government market do have our own language and are loathe to explain it to the uninitiated. And part is because it is easier for many to think they can't play in this market rather than to work at getting in the market. It's always easier to complain than to act. But if you come into this market without some education, beware. It's like the line from a Mary Chapin Carpenter song: *"Sometimes you're the windshield, sometimes you're the bug."* Most turn out to be the bug, as they expect market entry to be quick, seamless, simple and lucrative.

I receive calls almost daily from companies wanting to enter the government market. Although I don't have a standard response yet (I've only been doing this 20 years), I'm working on one. I try to explain that the market is big enough to accommodate many, but there are rarely "quick hit" new entries.

Many seem to believe if you get a GSA Schedule, you can sit back and wait for the phone to ring. Recently in a D.C. paper there was a listing for a seminar with the title "How to Get Your GSA Schedule and Make Your Cash Register Ring"! As *if* a Schedule was a cure-all — tell that to the hundreds of Schedule holders with $0 in sales.

The level of voluntary ignorance is staggering.

Everyone is looking for the easy way, the quick hit. The hardest point to get across is there is no single answer for every company — it all involves hard work and education. And then more of the same. This is an incremental market, near glacial in some respects.

And over the years, a number of half-truths, myths and

outright untruths have evolved and spread.

This introduction is an attempt to dispel a few of the misconceptions about selling to Fortune one — the U.S. Federal government. It will also prepare you for what follows, some real world lessons in what works when marketing to people who control some massive budgets.

MYTH 10: <u>It's too difficult to break into this market.</u>

Outside of Washington, D.C., outside the "beltway," D.C. is viewed as an insular world, full of intricacies, intrigue, insider partnerships, decoder rings and secret handshakes. In part, this is true. You need to know lots of things and lots of people to play in the arena of the mega-contracts, an arena dominated by Lockheed Martin, Northrop Grumman, Unisys and a handful of others.

These companies spend millions of dollars *bidding* on specific contracts, putting together the right team (subcontractors as well as key employees), following and influencing the direction of a contract as it evolves.

Most companies are not going to enter this arena without serious growing pains.

Does this mean you can't play here? Of course not. But you are not going to do it as a prime contractor. If you have the right product or service, and can offer some other significant "value-adds," there is always the role of sub-contractor, GSA Schedule vendor or selling in the open market.

And if you are a product vendor, start with the open market and develop some marketshare with targeted marketing efforts. *Then, and only then*, decide if you need to migrate to GSA Schedule, or some other contractual vehicles. Part of the decision-making process will be input from government prospects *asking* what contracts your product is on. Listen to them and make certain you have some way of collecting this data from your in-bound sales staff.

I have worked with over 100 companies that have developed strong marketshare exclusively through open market sales, as much as $20 million, with absolutely no contracts. It can be done, given a definable audience, a product that lends itself to micropurchase (under $2,500 per order), and a company skilled at selling and delivering at this level.

The real key to successful market entry is a good understanding of the real landscape before coming in. Does the government buy what you sell? If so, who are the current sellers (your competition)? What seems to be the preferred buying method (GSA Schedule, other contract, open market), and what can you offer that might differentiate you from the competition?

Understand these and you've got a chance at success.

MYTH 9: <u>The government demands the lowest price.</u>

For years this was a mantra, especially for companies selling through the GSA Schedule, and there is still a grain of truth to it. But the government only gets the best price in certain instances. A *competitive* price is necessary, but there are other factors that can influence the sale.

Quick delivery is a major differentiator, especially for products. If an employee needs a product today or tomorrow, delivery and a competitive price win. Not the best price, but a competitive price, and quick delivery.

Other factors, like quality, reputation, and customer service also play a role here, each with greater or lesser influence on each sale.

Nobody is saying this is easy, but the potential returns are huge.

If you accept this, your chances of success are already improving.

MYTH 8: <u>We have a great product; resellers will line up to sell our stuff</u>.

The calls I get from some manufacturers crack me up. "I hear you know the CEO of GTSI, get me in to see him and I'll give you a finder's fee."

There are *always* great products. I've never had a call from someone who had an average or crappy product. They're all great! **But there has to be more**. Will *your* marketing drive sales to your reseller partner? Can you supply your reseller with market development funds (a.k.a. "co-op dollars")? Are you already a commercial success? Is there a definable audience in the government for your product whose needs are not currently being met? Or is the incumbent vulnerable for other reasons?

What do you bring to the table aside from the product?

Define these, and your chances of success are looking better.

MYTH 7: <u>A GSA Schedule ("number") makes the cash register ring.</u>

Selling exclusively through the GSA Schedule is myopic and rarely leads to significant marketshare. And it brings significant headaches to those who are not fully prepared. Infrastructure issues are critical, but will not be addressed here.

Suffice it to say the top 5% of GSA Schedule vendors take 50% of all Schedule dollars. Why? Because they understand targeted marketing. They know how to play the game.

If you understand that the GSA Schedule is not a *cornucopia*, and that targeted marketing is required, your chances of success are getting even better.

MYTH 6: We can send press releases to the government publications and reporters will call.

This is akin to planning your retirement by purchasing lottery tickets. Every Tom, Dick and Harry faxes press releases to virtually every publication, and the government trade press is no different. Yes, being written about is important. But understand that everyone else is vying for attention, too.

Every morning at each publication someone comes in first and thumbs through the several inch stack of releases at the fax machine to see if something important is there. If not, it goes into the trash. Each reporter does the same thing, very quickly, in their e-mail.

Expecting a reporter to read a press release is not realistic. Expecting an editor to read a press release is less so. It is important to understand what each reporter writes about. Then specifically target your message to them, as an individual, with something newsworthy.

When—and if—a reporter or editor calls, they will have very specific questions, and will most likely have nothing to do with the reams of paper you or your PR firm faxed or e-mailed.

When you start getting press, your chances of success are getting real.

MYTH 5: <u>Our brand name recognition will drive sales in the government market</u>.

Brand is important, and a strong name can help. But it is not a guarantee. Dell dominates the desktop in government, but Dell wasn't DELL when it started selling to the government. Dell was small back then and it grew in this market in tandem with its overall growth (including BtoC and BtoB), and all of Dell's growth was incremental. Dell had a good product, good support, good marketing, and incremental growth. They also bothered to learn along the way. It did not hurt that the Dell business model fit perfectly with the procurement reforms of the early and middle 1990s.

Assuming the brand carries over is almost as laughable as "our corporate ad agency can do government." Most national

MYTH 2: <u>We'll hire a guy in D.C. and give it six months</u>.

This short-term commitment reflects a voluntary ignorance of the market that is inexcusable. And oddly enough, this happens with hundreds of companies each year. The reasons vary, but often include these elements: a person is hired who looks good on paper, sounds good in person, but who hasn't really delivered in their career. You hire someone who just left the government after 20+ years as a procurement or contracting officer—someone who may be able to exploit a few relationships, but who has a totally different skills set from what you really need.

Hiring the wrong person and giving them a limited window of opportunity is the kiss of death. Hiring the right person with the same window of opportunity isn't much better. Understanding that getting into this market isn't a short-term process is critical, as critical as hiring the right people. Do that and you're almost there.

m

wi

Yo

hak

fror

MYTH 1: <u>The biggest myth is a self-imposed limitation:</u> <u>*it's too big and we can't do it*</u>.

In my career I have worked with catalog businesses as small as a couple million in sales. Given time, we have helped several of these evolve into $20 million dollar companies with 30% of their sales in the public sector—open market sales.

I want to emphasize that the government market—federal, state and local—represents 25% of the Gross National Product, 20 million employees, and purchases buy every legitimate business product and service imaginable. But the market is comprised of a quagmire of niches—and the marketing approach that one size fits all *does not work*. Some companies are designed to sell direct on the open market, others more attuned to the channel approach, while some are natural subcontractor material. Some companies need GSA Schedules and others do not.

Get some legitimate guidance before entering this most lucrative of markets.

You are starting that process right here, right now.

About the Author

I have been working in the B2G (business-to-government) market for over 20 years. Amtower & Company began in 1985 as a custom list compiler. In 1989, one of my clients said, "What's great about talking to you is you never send me a bill." The consulting side was born. Since then, I have consulted with over 150 companies.

In 1991, I added public seminars. Since that time, I have produced over fifty events, including three conferences, with over 5,000 attendees. I am also a frequent presenter at other seminars and conferences. In the past two years I have made public and private presentations in over 20 states. I have served on the Board of Advisors for the major Federal trade shows, FOSE (still with us) and eGov (recently deceased).

Since I added consulting to my services, I have worked directly with literally hundreds of companies representing a broad range of products and services. My clients have included audio visual suppliers, footwear, air activated hand and foot warmers, computers and all manner of IT products and services, office supplies, shipping supplies, promotional products, publications, events, specialty paper companies, office furniture, training and education, recreational and restaurant equipment—you name it, I've probably advised a company or two. These companies have ranged in size from Fortune 50 to companies under 25 employees. Every company that has heeded my advice has prospered.

During that same period I have written for, been quoted by, and been written about in over 20 marketing and business publications. My e-newsletters are read by over 200,000 professionals each month.

I am an active participant in and student of this market, and I work hard at it.

This book is born out of a seminar that has been produced over 25 times publicly and a dozen or so times privately between 2002 and 2004. It has been revised a number of times since the first session on March 2002, and will continue to be updated as time permits. By all accounts, it is an excellent seminar, and many attend annually. The book also includes material previously published in *The Amtower B2G Market Report* and some of my *Off-White Papers*.

This book is designed to provide any company with an arsenal of tactics to use when targeting federal buyers via contract, GSA schedule, blanket purchase agreement, or open market. *None of this is brain surgery.* What this book is *not* is a sales manual on how to *sell* to the government, nor is it a book on how to do *contracting* with the government. *This book is about marketing tactics,* and is filled with stories to drive home the concepts presented. It will cover web marketing, customer relations, PR and press relations, events, direct marketing — snail mail and e-mail, space advertising, special interest groups associations, and some other things along the way. It is not necessarily linear.

All of these tactics are important, but each tactic may not fit your needs. Select those which suit your niche, your budget, and the talents of your staff.

You don't have to spend like Dell to grow in this market. And remember, when Dell started in this market in the early 1990s, it did not have the same budget it enjoys today. I know. I helped.

Last, but not least, I am not necessarily a great marketer, but I am a long-time student of marketing and the government market. In this, I have few peers, not because I have extraordinary insights, although on occasion I do. More because I have focused on one market, and have done it with a broad variety of products and services. My clients have afforded me the opportunity to offer advice on nearly the entire spectrum of business products and services over the past 20 years.

This book offers no magic pill. I have no "one size fits all" formula for success in the government market. I do not believe this exists. Nor does this book offer new, "breakthrough" marketing innovations. I am a firm believer that there are few, if any, new marketing ideas in the universe. There is what works, and there is what doesn't work. Both, under different circumstances, can be reshaped to fit the needs of any or all of us.

It all involves work.

So in this book, look for ideas you have seen elsewhere, but look at how they apply to the government marketplace, and more specifically — to you. I have borrowed ideas and concepts from a variety of sources over the years, and have used them for myself, my clients, my seminars, and now, my book. I will give credit where I can.

Let me know what you think at www.GovernmentMarketingBestPractices.com.

Mark Amtower

November, 2004

CHAPTER ONE

Fortune One: The U.S. Federal Government

You will be successful in this market when the players in the market (vendors and government customers) think of your company, your product, your service, when your market niche is a topic of discussion. This occurs when you have successfully become pervasive in your niche without being invasive, annoying. When key players think positively of your company, they will be more comfortable and more likely to mention your company in settings where it will do the most good.

The government market was brought into focus for me in the mid-1990s. One evening I was watching *Entertainment Tonight* when Leonard Maltin (the movie critic) came on. He was very excited because Hollywood had just broken the $5 billion barrier for movie ticket sales. Wow—ticket sales over $5 billion! As we all know, Hollywood gets lots of press, has lots of glitz and glamour, and has the attention of the American public on an all too regular basis.

I found this tidbit intriguing, but not for the same reason Mr. Maltin did.

This fact put things in perspective for me because one of the contracts that I was consulting on at that time — the SuperMini contract — was worth an estimated $9-11 billion dollars. *The government market is only sexy if you like money.* Hollywood may have the glamour and the glitz, but if you want to play in the big leagues, the world's biggest market, you better start learning about business-to-government marketing.

Everything else is small by comparison.

There are over 80,000 governments in the United States, counting the Federal government as one, and each state government as one. There are over 30,000 townships, over 30,000 municipalities, over 3,000 counties, over 14,000 special district governments, and over 500 Indian tribes. These represent more than 20,000,000 employees, so be careful where you tell those "close enough for government work" jokes. The U.S. Federal government is considered to be "Fortune One," representing a huge portion of our national economy. Many state governments would qualify for Fortune 100. Over three hundred thousand companies are registered to do business with the Federal government, representing the Fortune 500 down to – literally – Mom & Pop shops.

The stakes are high and it is a complicated game. If you come in expecting it to be easy, you will be in for a rude surprise.

On the other hand, if you are willing to learn, and understand the incremental – and niche- nature of this market, you have a good chance at surviving and thriving.

Current Situation

Being proactive is still the best way to be successful. Here is the current landscape:

- there are more players, many of them new players

- the SmartPay card, the small purchase card for government in FY '03, contributed 16.2 billion dollars in sales. This will be about 17.5 billion in FY '04.

- the GSA schedule continues to grow. The IT schedule alone in FY '03 was roughly $15 billion. The total GSA schedules, all 54 Schedules at the time, produced approximately 26 billion dollars in sales.

- the IT Schedule, Schedule 70, has approximately 4,800 of the 10,000 or so GSA Schedule holders.

Additionally there are literally hundreds of contracts out there, including blanket purchase agreements (BPAs), agency-

3

specific contracts, and government-wide acquisition contracts, GWACs. The market as a result is much more competitive than ever before. There are more players, more contracts, and more confusion than in years past. And advertising clutter only adds to this confusion. So your mission—your assignment, Mr. Phelps, if you will—is to **make your company stand out and stand apart** from all the clutter and all the confusion in this market. That being the case, Amtower's First Law is:

> ****Positive mindshare managed proactively leads to growth in marketshare.****

But there is no single path to develop this mindshare and to manage it proactively. If you are unsure about the concept of "mindshare," I strongly recommend *Positioning: The Battle for Your Mind*, by Al Ries and Jack Trout. It is an older book with dated examples, but well-worth the time.

To grow mindshare, we have to fight through all of the other messages out there. In 2000 Victor Hunter wrote a book called *Business-to-Business Direct Marketing – Creating Community of Customers*. This is another book worth your time. One of his major tenets in this book was that prospects require 12 to 18 contacts per year to convert to customers, and customers require 24 to 36 contacts per year for retention. The contact methods included mail, telephone, fax, e-mail, web visits, radio, in-person sales call, booth visits, space ads, and on and on. It didn't matter as long as there was a customer touch somewhere in that process. If this is accurate, then the second of several Amtower's laws that will apply here is:

Amtower's Second Law: Marketing is the art of being repetitive without being boring, becoming pervasive in your niche without being invasive in your tactics.

There is too much "noise" in the world, and advertising simply adds to that noise. It doesn't mean you should do less, or more, it means that that you should do it better and smarter, targeting those most likely to like and need what you do. Which leads to a major premise for marketshare growth: *It is critical to define and identify your core target audience to grow the marketshare.*

You have to know *who* in government are your significant buyers and influencers, and specifically target these people. This involves a significant amount of research (and I assume it is done). You should start by looking at your own customer database to see who (by job function) buys from you, and which agencies they are in. You can make some assumptions based on this data as to what other agencies might be potential buyers.

5

Once the research is done, and you know where the buyers are, you need to determine a couple other things. First, who these customers are currently buying from (if not you) and who your competitors are. Secondly, you need to determine how the customers prefer to buy your product or service: GSA, open market, or some other contract.

Most companies will want to expand their presence *immediately*. These companies assume at this point that a frontal assault is best to grow marketshare—just start going head-to-head with the incumbent. Often, this is advice from an advertising agency, operating on the premise that broader advertising will result in increased sales.

I disagree, which leads to Amtower's Third Law:

> *** It is possible to significantly grow marketshare by maximizing sales to your installed customer base.***

This involves the "R" word – the ability to establish and maximize the value of *relationships.*

We've seen this time and time again when a company has a foothold in one agency. Senior management will decide to prospect across the government rather than to grow marketshare in the one agency where they are obviously already liked and where their product or service is already known. It's much easier to grow on an incremental basis where people already know and like you than to try to prospect across the vast government market. "Owning" an agency is critical to maintaining and building marketshare. If you are in this position, decide to dominate as much as possible in that one agency before you migrate to new agencies.

Incremental growth is sane and do-able. Spending money on prospecting in new agencies before your beachhead is established is, at best, risky and can spread your resources too thin.

Remember Arnold

When Mr. Schwartzenegger came to this country, I believe in the 1970s, he went to Hollywood and got an interview with an agent. The agent's advice, "Lose the accent, change your name." Mr. Schwartzenegger did not care for, or follow, this advice. He made Pumping Iron, *which became a cult classic, without doing either. Though I've not seen it, I understand there is not much in the way of dialogue, but it is sort of a lift, grunt, flex documentary. His next movie that I recall was "Conan," which was pretty much the same movie—lift, grunt and flex—but he was wearing a tutu. Ever-expanding circles. Slowly out of that, he evolved into action movies, into comedy, and into politics. But he did it on an incremental basis, slowly over time, building a fan base for each as he went along. There was no single big moment, just continuous momentum.*

What does this mean for you? If you are coming into this market looking for a big hit, really fast growth, look elsewhere. If you think you are the exception (and *many* have thought this), let's look at a couple of examples.

In the early 1980s, Exxon, in its infinite wisdom, entered the B2B and B2G markets with Exxon Office Systems. Does anyone, except for a few of the people still in this market who worked there, remember this? Exxon assumed that its brand name would "wow" the potential customer base, open some doors, and create cash flow. It just didn't happen, and Exxon Office Systems disappeared almost as quickly as it emerged. Apparently no one was going to buy "office systems" from a gas station. Although this oversimplifies the situation, it is basically accurate.

Another example of *"Here I am, give me your money"* is General Electric. Bohdan Associates was an early computer reseller in the B2G market, and they were successful in the middle 1980s. The Bohdan name recognition was good, the relationship they had with Compaq was great, and growth was solid, if not spectacular. Then in the early 1990s, Bohdan was purchased by Ameridata. Ameridata apparently had some presence in the B2B world, but no name recognition with government buyers. So naturally the first thing Ameridata did was drop the Bohdan name, immediately confusing the customers. Within two years, along comes GE Capital and buys Ameridata. Someone at GE Capital had been paying attention to the growth in the B2G computer market, and they wanted "in." So GE Capital bought Ameridata.

The first thing GE did was change the name from Ameridata to General Electric (GE) Capital Information Technology (IT) Federal Solutions: GE Capital IT Federal Solutions. (Think Donald Sutherland from *The Dirty Dozen:* "Very pretty, Colonel, but can they fight?"). Could there be a longer name for a company? Inside of a couple years, customers comfortable with the good service they had been getting from Bohdan were doubly confused by two name changes. This being the government market, I created a name out of the acronym and starting referring to them as GEE-Sit-Fiz.

Say it with me once: GEEEsitFIZZ. It isn't often you get to make fun of GE, so let's savor the moment.

GE/Ameridata/Bohdan folded. And it didn't have to happen.

It doesn't matter who you are, growth in this market is incremental, even if you have a really big name. Be prepared for the long haul and incremental growth.

Companies that are big players in this market have been doing this a long time, and their growth has been incremental. They also understand how to take advantage of the changing landscape. Throughout the late 1980s and early 1990s, GTSI was the dominant vendor on Schedule 70, the information technology Schedule. The emergence of Dell, and later the addition of services to Schedule 70, ended that dominance.

Let's take a look at the top IT vendors of 2004.

Top Schedule 70 Vendors 2004

- Dell
- IBM
- NGIT
- Booz Allen
- SAIC

- Motorola
- EDS
- Oracle
- GTSI
- Accenture

We have Dell (9%), IBM (2.73%), Northrop (2.41%), Booz Allen (2.26%), Science Applications (2.13%), Motorola (1.85%), EDS (1.76%), Oracle (1.76%), GTSI (1.51%) and Accenture (1.40%). The top Schedule vendors represent the companies that truly dominate dollar-wise the GSA schedule. Top suppliers by unaided name recognition, according to Market Connections' 2003 study:

Top Suppliers by <u>Unaided</u> Name Recognition

Market Communications Study

- Dell 76%
- CDW-G 47%
- H-P 42%
- GTSI 38%
- Microsoft 31%

- IBM 28%
- Cisco 18%
- GovConnection 8%
- CompUSA 7%
- NGIT 5%

These included number one, Dell at 76 percent, CDW at 47 percent, GTSI at 38 percent. This is the first time that CDW-G had passed GTSI in the four years this study has been done. CDW-G and GTSI are both major resellers in the government market space. A few years back CDW-G was barely on the radar scope, and they have worked hard at moving up, and have done so incrementally.

Each of these top suppliers has visibility (read "mindshare") promoted by a combination of orchestrated marketing methods. The methods include the things we'll be talking about to a large extent: space, web, events, direct, e-mail, telemarketing, press relations and public relations, customer relations, special interest groups, associations, and more.

But not all of the vendors mentioned, nor all of the successful vendors mentioned, use the same marketing mix. Budgetary and staff considerations often intervene. The audience each vendor is trying to reach determines much of the mix. If it is a large, diffuse audience, you have one set of tactics. If it is a small, targeted group, you have another. That being the case, another major premise is *by delivering a variety of messages to a carefully defined audience on a regular basis, you can create positive mindshare.*

And Amtower's Fourth Law is a direct corollary to this:

> ***Sending the same stuff over and over will irritate people.***

But the same core message(s) can be delivered in a variety of ways, including direct mail, snail mail, telemarketing, live sales calls — any number of contact methods.

Understanding the Players

This is a mobile, and to an extent, inbred community, on both the government and vendor side, so relationships count. There's a lot of mobility inside government with senior executives, in particular IT executives, and mid-level IT players specifically. These are people who migrate within agency and from agency to agency to facilitate their career path. This will be more important and more obvious the year after an election. Over the past decade or so we have seen more migration from government to industry than before.

At the Office of Personnel Management web site (www.opm.gov), you can obtain statistical data on Federal employment (click on FedScope): age, sex, minority and veteran employment, geographic, how many employees in which agency, and the like. This is always important information to have access to, so visit this site a couple times each year to make sure you are current, or subscribe to the OPM newsletter which will inform you of changes in the data.

Among the important trends: the Federal workforce is aging. The Senior Executive Service (SES), the career executives in all the Federal agencies, averages 55 years old, and many are eligible for retirement. The overall average age of Federal employees is 47. These are factors to consider when writing your marketing materials: we are not writing for a younger audience.

On the vendor side, I am unaware of statistical information. We often see people switching companies for a variety of similar reasons, especially among systems integrators and those involved in selling information technology. So it's a very mobile community, but the players remain largely the same — you just have to know where they are and where they are going.

But, the relationships truly count. By this I am referring to multiple levels of relationships. If you do business by partnering on larger contracts, you need to develop relationships at the executive level, at the business development level, and have direct relationships with the influencers on the government side. If you are simply selling products and services directly to an agency, your sales staff needs to have relationships with the buyers and influencers inside the agencies.

Where and how do you develop and maintain the relationships that you have with your vendor partners, as well as with your government customers?

On the government side, you have to understand that career federal employees take pride in their work, probably more now than ever before. When you are developing a relationship, knowing simple things like "on time, on budget" makes your client — your government customer — a star, is critical. It makes any customer a star, but particularly in this market. If you deliver, they will remember. And if you do not deliver, they will remember. The "hot buttons" of government employees are not totally different than their consumer counterparts, but *how they buy* and *how these purchases are reviewed* are different. Therein lie the nuances.

Federal managers migrate annually at about a 15 percent rate, and this will spike to more than 30 percent in the year following an election, regardless of the election results. All government buyers (indeed, everyone) rely on peers for vendor information, so it is absolutely critical that you have in place some sort of program that encourages your buyers to talk about your company, your products, your services to their peers. And all government employees — federal, state, local, it doesn't really matter — feel that government needs are different from "business." Regardless of the validity of this, you have to acknowledge this in as many ways as you can, using government jargon, having special web sites for the government people, using the SmartPay logo, and many other things.

This became clear in the mid-to-late 1990s when CDW came into the government market. CDW is a large IT catalog company. They came in with a single government and education catalog: CDW-E/G Government and education buy the same way, but they are two distinct entities, and both of them believe that they have vastly different needs. It wasn't

16

until CDW segmented the government catalog from the education catalog that they truly started to make significant inroads in both markets. CDW acknowledged the differences and started addressing them separately, and successfully.

In the earlier years of government IT contracting (1970s and 1980s), courteous service was rare, as a few vendors had a lock on the market. Government buyers, though, are like any other customers. Prompt, courteous service has evolved as a major differentiator in recent years, especially since the B2B catalogers have discovered the government market and brought in their vastly superior customer service on the product side of the universe. Once again, we see that Federal buyers are not dissimilar from their consumer counterparts — everyone likes good customer service.

So the first line of your defense, then, is who answers the phone? Does anyone answer the phone in your organization? If you have one of those silly voice prompt systems, how many people are going to drop off the phone before they even get through the menu?

What It Takes To Be a Player

Many of the companies in the government marketplace sell only to the government because they understand the nuances well enough to be a significant player in certain niches without needing to go out into the broader B-to-B or business-to-consumer universe. This is true for each product or service category, but let's take a look at those 4,800 or so companies that are currently on the IT GSA Schedule, Schedule 70.

The real growth here is occurring primarily among *the few proactive marketers and vendors*. These companies dominate. Remember, we're talking about over $15 billion in FY 2004 just on Schedule 70.

FY 2003 Schedule 70

- Dell – 9%

- Top 5 – 19%

- Top 10 – 25%

- Top 50 – 55%

- Top 100 – 67%

- Top 2½ % take 67%

Dell, all by itself, took 9 percent of that $15 billion or so. The top five vendors took 19 percent, the top 10, 25 percent.

The top 50 took 55 percent and the top 100 took two-thirds, 67 percent. Two-and-a-half percent of the vendors on Schedule 70 took two-thirds of the 14 billion or so that was spent.

The second tier — we'll call those number 101 to number 3,000 or so — took 28 percent, roughly low eight figures to high five figures. The bottom tier, the next 1,800 or so companies, took the remaining five percent of the dollars. Pocket change. Several hundred of these companies made zero dollars on their schedule.

This applies across the board. We ran the numbers for several Schedules, such as Schedule 51, the walk-in, walk-out hardware category. There were only 13 companies on Schedule 51, but one company took 50 percent of the $5 million dollars from that Schedule.

What is the difference? The difference is intelligent, proactive marketing — *identifying* the prospects and *creating* the opportunities, *developing* the relationships, and developing the right approach for your niche predicated on customer feedback. Keep in mind the idea that no two paths have to be the same. There are many paths here. You don't have to spend advertising dollars like Dell to grow marketshare.

Amtower's Three Questions

In order to better understand who your customers are, three questions stand out in my mind:

> *1 - What do you read?*
>
> *2 - What do you attend?*
>
> *3- What do you belong to?*

The more niche you are, the more narrow your product or service area, the more important these answers are going to be to you. You don't have to reach everybody in the government universe if you understand where the vast majority of *your* customers and prospects get their information, either by publication, by event, or by association affiliation.

So right now, we'll look at some statistical information, courtesy of our friends at Market Connections. This is an annual study on the buying habits of senior IT managers in the Federal government, but we believe the many factors carry over to any product or service category.

Factors Considered When Deciding on a Supplier

- Quality of products and services

- Customer service and support

- Ability to resolve problems

- Staff has right skills and knowledge

- Thoroughness of work performed

- On schedule delivery

Customers rated the above factors in this order: 1) the quality of products and services; 2) the ability to resolve problems; 3) the thoroughness of the work performed; 4) customer service and support; 5) your staff has the right skills and knowledge; 6) on schedule delivery. This is actually the first year that customer service wasn't number one, and this is the fourth year of the study. But the ability to resolve problems, and customer service and support, are very much the same type customer service issue.

Once you determine what the most important traits are, and where you fit in that arena, you should be able to develop an action list to improve areas of weakness. The traits most important to your niche may vary from these, or show up in a different order. Those responsible for fleet management in government may find fast delivery and quality products to be the most critical issues, while those in administrative positions may need more problem solving assistance.

Next we look at the ***information grazing habits*** of your customers. How do your customers and prospects gather information to make their buying decisions? How do they determine which product best suits their needs as well as which vendor to provide it? Again, the more "niche" you are, the more the three questions come into play.

The objective is to determine the right marketing mix for your company: what efforts on your part will create the most ***gravitational pull*** for your company in your niche. You have to fight through all the noise in the marketplace to create enough mindshare to be at or near top of mind when your product/service niche comes up in conversation, or when a need for a product or service in your area arises in a government office.

*****Gravitational pull*** is the players in the market thinking of your company, your product, your service when your market niche is a topic of discussion. This occurs when you have successfully become pervasive in your niche without being invasive, annoying.*

When key players think positively of your company, they will be more comfortable and more likely to mention your company in settings where it will do the most good.

Information Sources Used

- Web sites
- Articles

- Colleagues
- E-mail

- Other agencies
- User groups

- Space ads
- E-newsletters

- Sales reps
- Catalogs

- Seminars
- Direct mail

- Trade shows, in-agency shows

Copyright 2004, Market Connections

1) web site; 2) colleagues; 3) other agencies; 4) trade shows and in-agency events; 5) sales rep; 6) seminars; 7) articles; 8) e-mail; 9) user groups; 10) e-newsletters; 11) catalogs; 12) direct mail; and last but not least, 13) space advertising.

Of the information sources used, according to Market Connections, the number one information source is the **web**.

It's been the web for a couple of years. The first time it showed up was year two of the study with a narrow margin over "colleagues." The margin has been widening ever since.

Everybody goes to the web first for information. "Googled" is now a verb. We can assume that a lot of people think the information available on the web will be unbiased, but we know that's not true.

The Market Connections study is research that involves people, not simply government employees, so we offer a grain of salt here. None of us likes to believe that advertising, catalogs, direct mail, e-mail influences us. The truth is each of those factors influence us to greater or lesser degrees. It's just that very few of us will readily admit it. But all of it does influence us.

So, web sites — and I agree — is number one, and colleagues is number two. These results have been pretty constant since Market Connections has been doing this study. So the elements we'll discuss, starting with the next chapter: web marketing, customer relations, PR and press relations, events, seminars, direct mail, e-mail, space advertising, special interest groups and associations along the way.

CHAPTER TWO

The Web

Survey says, number one influencer, three years in a row. Why should you push the web? It is your first face forward, the first impression many will get of your company. First impressions are absolutely critical here as they are anywhere. This means you should need a very proactive and informational web site.

Before you read any further, think about your favorite web site(s). Why do you like this/these site(s)? What are the attributes you find most appealing and useful? List three of them now, and compare these attributes to your company web site.

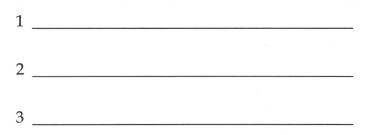

For me, my favorite site where I buy is Amazon. It is easy to use, easy to find things and buy things. And each time I look for a particular book, the site shows me other books people buy when they have purchased that book. My favorite informational sites are the publications (www.fcw, www.gcn.com, www. washingtontechnology.com, www.catalogagemag.com, and others)—at least those that do not charge to access past issues.

This is where people get their first impressions of you. If you have pages that perpetually say, "Under construction," or if your site seems to have dated information, this creates a negative impression on the people you are trying to influence. The likelihood of return visits from these people is slight.

You and your company are obviously out of the mainstream if you are not setting the web site as the major priority. All too often I hear, "Well, our web site update is next on our 'to do' list." Next is not good enough. Now is the time to act, right this minute.

Step one is to determine what the *goals* are for your web site. Is it to...

- *attract* new visitors?

- keep each visitor *longer*?

- get each to visit *more often*?

- get them to *inquire and buy*?

- get them to *tell their peers* about your web site?

- get them to *sign up* for your newsletter?

Maybe all of the above? What are *your* major goals for your site? Before you can build a successful site, you need to know what you want it to do, and you need to know what the technical and emotional drivers are so you can create a web site that works for you.

What are your initial goals:

1 _____

2 _____

3 _____

4 _____

According to Market Connections, the government buyers feel that features of a good government facing web site include:

Features of a Good Web Site

- Current, accurate information

- Clear presentation

- Pricing information

- Easy navigation

- Loads quickly

- Well indexed

- Good search engine

- Good links

- No ads or banners

- *Good response mechanism

- *Real news

So what do we have: first, *current accurate information*. This means a web site that is informationally updated and checked for accuracy on a regular basis. Old information sends an unsubtle message that you are lazy, or that you don't care.

Second is a *clear presentation* — don't clutter every web page. When you see "white space" it doesn't mean that it has to be filled.

Number three reminds us there should be current *pricing* information. Often I hear the argument that a company doesn't want to make it easy for a competitor to see the pricing. The web site is for your *customer*, and if they cannot find what they want, the likelihood is they will not call for pricing, but move to another web site. If the pricing varies by contract, say so

Fourth is *easy navigation*, which shows up on every survey for any market. The site has to be easy to get around. A general rule is "three clicks:" three clicks to find anything and to get in and out. The most trafficked web sites are those that are easy to navigate, and that have things worth looking at.

Number five is interesting: the site has to *load quickly*. This is a simple rule that often gets left behind with each new "flash" or similar web gizmo used as the "introduction" page for a web site. We have all been to sites that require a new version of Flash ("click here to always trust Macromedia"). This feature causes a slower loading time, and if the "skip into" button isn't easy to see, many people will drop off before the introduction fully loads. In a technical aside: techies do not design intuitive web sites. Do not let your techies run rampant by adding all of the latest bells and whistles to your web site. Too much flash will lead to very little, if any, cash.

Sixth is your site should be *well indexed,* relating back to the three click rule. Good indexing invariably leads to longer visits with more page views. The longer someone stays at your site the more likely it is they will be back, and perhaps, purchase from you.

Number seven, have a *good search engine,* also related numbers four and six.

Number eight, *good links.* Bad links reflect on you. There are web services that test your links, but whoever is in charge of your web site should be doing this. The larger the site, the more difficult this becomes, so third party services are often the answer.

Number nine, *banners and ads* have been a distraction. Early on, in the late 1990s, they were hot. Then in the early 2000s they cooled off and people said they didn't like them. The tide is turning again. You might want to test these, as the general web-world seems to be migrating back toward banners. Pop-up ads are a different matter. I personally do not like them at all, but there are strong feelings both ways.

The last two items here are my thoughts, not part of the Market Connections survey. There has to be a *good response mechanism* on *every page* of the web site. Without a good response mechanism, the best information in the world just doesn't mean anything. Customers and prospects have to be able to *get in touch with you*. Put your 800 number on each page, and put an e-mail address where they can contact somebody quickly.

Many sites are now using the icon that says "click here to speak with somebody live on the web." Often this has a picture of someone with a headset on. This shows up at the Hewlett-Packard government site, among others. I don't know if it shows up on the H-P B-to-B site, but it is a very, very strong component of the H-P government site.

The last item that I would add to this list would be to *post real news*. Your press releases most likely aren't getting published anywhere, so why not post them at your web site and create mini-news stories around them? This affords you the opportunity to refresh your site regularly and to tell your own story.

There are other ways to have current news at your web site.

Most of the major trade publications license stories to vendors for posting. You can link to the stories for free, but that takes the visitor off your site, which you do *not* want to do. If you find a story that highlights your company or your niche and mentions your product favorably, license the story from the publication. The fee is minimal and it will keep your site more informationally robust.

Other good web site features — these are Amtower features, not Market Connections — you've got to have a government section for your web site. It simply has to be there. You can develop white papers or other position papers for downloading information that helps people make buying decisions. You can take your press releases and develop news items about them, about your company, about your niche. If you sell enough products, you can do what has kept David Letterman top of mind for many people, develop a *top ten list* and show the top ten products or services that the government is buying. If you have enough bandwidth, enough government traction and sales, you can do it by DoD and civilian, because they might be different.

Further web site features: if you have multiple contracts, you should have a page for each contractual vehicle, with contract-specific news coming from the contracting agency, the contracting officer, as well as contract news from the trade publications. You can have reciprocal

government agencies that own the contract

credit card logo all over, especially wherev

Mastercard and Visa card logos.

You've all been to sites where there is an "e-mail this page to a friend" button. "E-mail this page to a colleague" could be a significant way for people in government to share information about products, services and companies they like. On your homepage, your "mycompany.com/gov" homepage, have a button there (don't make them to do control-D) which says, *"Click here to make this your homepage."* Offer it to them. Not many people are going to take you up on this, but for those that do, your site opens up on their computer every time they log on. The more niche-specific information your offer, the more likely some people will take advantage of it.

Links are important. The more links you have, the higher you are in search engines. I would also suggest to you that using Google, Overture, and any other services out there for search engine optimization (SEO) has become very important. Buying key words and phrases has become crucial in the "click wars."

You can purchase links and other advertising at the various trade publications. There are also ways to get links at government sites. Government will not link to you without a t of arm-twisting. Agencies are not supposed to endorse cific vendors, but if you have a contract with an agency, then the contracting officer has a vested interest in your success because more dollars through that contract vehicle justifies their existence. So if you approach the contracting officer, you'll probably get a web link on the contract page of agency site.

Association and special interest group (SIG) sites often have links to vendors. I suggest that you join those associations and SIGs most pertinent to your niche and make certain that you have an active web link there. Remember the *Three Questions*. Special interest groups can represent significant groups of influencers.

There are some informational sites on the web that may be beneficial if they have enough traffic. www.PublicWorks.com, www.Govfacility.com and others target very specific groups in the public sector.

Don't forget links at your business partners, the companies with whom you do business. The more links you have, the higher your visibility, the higher up your results are on search engines.

Site maintenance issues should include making certain that your web site pages print. Often you'll try to print a web page and it truncates either on the right side or y

pages come out just short. If you can print

it will be much better, because governmer

pages out of catalogs and they will print p

to share with their coworkers at various meetings. If your page

does not print cleanly, it may be missing contact or pricing

information that would be important. The point is simple:

make sure that your web pages print cleanly.

You can also monitor www.google.com/unclesam for any

news about your company and competitors. Most people

use google.com, and most people do not know about google.

com/unclesam. This portion of Google views only government

web sites—federal, state, and local. This is a way you can see

what government agencies are saying about you and your

competitors. You can also gather a variety of useful data using

this tool.

Seriously consider having that "click here" call button

which goes directly to a sales rep. If your rep knows the caller

is at your site, they have the opportunity to walk the caller

through your site, sort of a personal guided tour.

I monitor several sites on a regular basis. CDW-G is

one of the better sites, perhaps one of the best sites in the

b2government market (www.cdwg.com). It is easy to navigate,

locate products and shop.

...safety is also a very good site (www.labsafety.com).

...highlight special features for their government visitors. ...rom the front page — it's a little difficult to find it — but on the bottom right-hand corner, you find the "Resource Centers." The top one is government, which takes you to the Lab Safety government page.

"See why government buyers choose LabSafety.com" is the headline on the page. Seven or eight reasons are then clearly enunciated.

SmartPay welcome here

Real people answer the phone

Great product selection

...all things that government buyers are interested in, that they have said through the Market Connection studies that they want. Keep in mind that Lab Safety is *not* a GSA Schedule vendor, so they're appealing to the micro-purchasers, the under $2,500 per purchase credit card buyer, which is why they lead with the SmartPay.

At the bottom of the list of multiple reasons that Lab Safety has, they have "E-Z Facts Documents." Click on this and you get "great reference information about the products and issues that affect you in the public safety industry." EZ Facts takes certain parts of the Code of Federal Regulations (CFR) and shows where the CFR is endorsing the use of specific types of products. Lab Safety links these back to its own products. The CFR is not endorsing Lab Safety, per se, but CFR is endorsing the use of certain products. Lab Safety has cross-referenced their products with the CFR reference endorsing the use of these products by government employees. This is an extraordinary differentiator for a company that sells totally open market, and it offers the government buyers reasons to stay longer at the site. It also provides the government buyer with legitimate reasons and justification for making the purchase.

The publication sites, Federal Computer Week (www.fcw.com), Government Computer News (www.gcn.com), and Government Executive (www.govexec.com) are all very informationally robust sites, as you would expect from publications. There are ideas that you can borrow from these sites. Take a look at each, or the publications that best serve your niche, and get ideas for your site.

You might also want to get regular feedback from site visitors, but not just from *any* visitors that you have. The people that you most want feedback from are the people that spend money with you through your web site: real customers spending real money. If you simply put a survey up on your site, the people most likely to fill it out are people who have little else to do. You might want to put your survey in the shopping cart area, or use it as a follow-up in the e-mail order confirmation.

So, what are your top action items for your web re-design?

1 _____

2 _____

3 _____

4 _____

5 _____

CHAPTER THREE

Customer Relations and Creating Buzz

In 2000, Emmanuel Rosen wrote a largely overlooked book called *Creating Buzz*. This book should be examined closely. The book addresses the issue of how to create excitement around a product, service or company. Rosen offers many examples of how companies have used "buzz" via groups, the internet and other venues to create excitement around what your company is doing.

Earlier I mentioned that relationships are important in this market, and this will be a recurrent theme. Encouraging your best customers to talk about you is the point of this chapter.

The 80/20 rule, the Pareto Principle, says 80 percent of your revenue comes from 20 percent of your customers. I find this true with almost every company I have worked with, but the spread is more like 90/10

Do you know *who those 20 percent are for your company?* If you do, what are you doing to treat these people *differently*, like they truly deserve to be treated?

I have a prospect pyramid that is very different than many you may have seen. The middle portions are the same: advocate, customer, buyer, prospect, suspect. But at the very bottom, we have burn victim — people that hate your guts — and at the very top, we have apostles.

The Amtower Pyramid Prospect

- Apostle
- Advocate
- Customer
- Buyer
- Prospect
- Suspect
- Burn victim

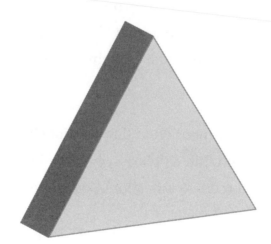

Copyright 2004, Amtower & Co.

Your pyramid is comprised of not just your customers and prospects. Your pyramid is comprised of the press, your vendor partners, your employees and former employees and any investors that you may have, either as a public company or as a private company. So you have a number of audiences that you have to be concerned about on a regular basis.

Each of these groups has the ability to influence others, often in significant ways. Knowing key members of each group and developing and managing relationships with each key player is consequential. The consequences can be good or bad, depending on how you manage the relationship.

At the top of this pyramid, we have the apostles — customers that rave about you. These are the best referral agents you could possibly have. These are people who love your product or service and they are natural allies. They also require recognition from you in some form, and hopefully on a regular basis. They are also people who, if burned by you, will fry you. There seems to be some historical precedent that with twelve of these people, you can do extraordinary things.

Your apostles and advocates are your key buyer groups, and not just because they spend money with you. The Market Connections study (page 33) ranks the major information sources, and "peer recommendation" is second. "Peer" may have dropped to number two on the influence list, but it is still very important.

Why should you treat your best customers differently? Why would you treat them differently? Isn't this an ethical gray area in the government market?

No, not if you do it right. Why do you treat them differently? Number one, because they deserve it. Number two, because you can. Number three, because you should. Number four, if you don't, someone else might—and if they do it better than you, the apostle/customer might migrate. And, number five, if you do all of the above—because they deserve it, because you can, because you should—when they speak about you, you will shine.

Steve Jobs at Apple has apostles, and he has had them since the early 1980s. These are people that rave about the Apple products, about the service they get from the company, about Steve Jobs being a minor deity in their universe. I am convinced his more rabid fans may have little "Steve altars" in their basements, with incense and candles and pictures of Mr. Jobs. The simple fact is that Apple—the company—has apostles and advocates—not in truly great numbers, but enough to keep the brand alive and profitable. Apple does not have huge marketshare, but they have huge mindshare with a devoted group of fans, people that really, really love the product. Most PC companies do not have advocates like this. Even Dell fans are not as rabid as Apple fans. There is even a publication called *Mac Addict*.

The likelihood of replicating the Apple apostle base is very small, because these people are truly dedicated to the platform. But you can identify your best customers and create programs to treat them better. **I recommend that 50 percent of your marketing budget be allocated specifically for apostle and advocate development and customer retention and marketing programs.** *Not for prospecting, but for customer retention. It costs much less to retain a good customer than to develop a new one.*

MPC (formerly Micron PC) has done this in productive ways. They own mindshare in a limited number of Federal agencies, so they concentrate their efforts on these agencies and their best customers within those agencies. At FOSE in 2003, they hosted a hospitality suite away from the show floor where their best customers were invited for refreshments and to relax. There was no selling in the hospitality suite – it was simply a way to say "thank you" to their best customers. The exit survey indicated that these people had never been treated this well at any event before. I am certain that MPC finds several ways to stay in touch with its best customers, and to continuously treat them well.

In 2004, it is also important to remember there that feds migrate, *especially* after an election. In a normal year, we see about 15% migration in the senior federal management community. This will spike to 30% or higher the year following an election. During 2005, there will be extraordinary migration, regardless of the election outcome, in the senior executive community in the federal government. Regionally, nationally, all over the federal government, there will be migration. If your product or service is sold at a high level, or needs approval at high levels, this is important to keep in mind. Using the Carroll *Federal Executive Directory* or similar directory would be useful for keeping current.

Customer acquisition costs keep going up. It is much easier to keep customers if you treat them right. It is also less expensive to keep customers than it is to acquire new ones. The acquisition mode means that you're weaning them away from a company that they prefer either in a proactive or a default mode. Remember the second law: you can significantly grow your marketshare by selling to your installed base. MPC owns mindshare in a limited number of federal agencies. They have grown their marketshare and stayed a very active and significant player in this market, not by trying to prospect by going head-to-head against Dell or Gateway or Hewlett-Packard, which would be very difficult for them. They have grown their mindshare in very specific agencies where they are already known, where they are already liked, and they treat these customers extraordinarily well. After an election, when some of their customers will move, there is always the possibility of MPC moving with them—retaining one account and gaining a new one.

44

Survey your best customers for their needs on a regular basis. Develop a special reward or recognition program for them. It could be as simple as always informing them first about a new product or service, or inviting them first to an event where you'll be exhibiting or presenting, or like MPC, having a hospitality suite. I like using the *Federal Personnel Guide*, but there have been occasions when there has been resistance among some sales people about this.

I have seen other instances where these principles are completely ignored. One egregious example is in a company I advised briefly. In this company, sales reps did not "own" accounts. When I asked why, it was explained that the management felt that if a sales representative had a relationship with the agency buyers, when the rep left the company the account would leave with him/her. This company also capped what a sales rep could earn, thereby guaranteeing migration of the better salespeople. Although extreme, this is a true story. This is an extreme example of bad sales and marketing practices compounded by a paranoid management team. It should be pointed out that it was a deservedly paranoid management team, but it was a situation they created themselves, and they continue to manage the same way, and have high turnover. This is a company that could well own a strong niche in the market, but its sales remain flat over the past four years as a result of poor management practices.

Sales reps should own specific accounts. People in agencies should be able to call the same person over and over again, whenever they want. There's a comfort level there, and there's a relationship that can be built there. Once the customer trusts his/her sales representative, the customer is happy with the service, the level and kind of information, and the great help — that customer is more likely to share *upcoming* needs so your company can develop and can create opportunities that would not otherwise become apparent. Time and again we have seen the relationship model work: witness MPC. Although it is usually easier with companies that sell via contract vehicles (GSA Schedule or other contract), it has also occurred with companies selling open market — no contracts at all.

Once you have established a program for treating your best customer properly, it is time to migrate other customers up the food chain. You have to be able to look in your database and identify more active buyers to move them up to the advocate and apostle stage. The Vic Hunter model (see page 20) would indicate that increasing contact with them is a good next step. You can also mix different offers for emerging agency customers or regular buyers. If you see an agency that could become one of your better customers, look at what they are buying and offer "spot reductions" to gain marketshare. Just make sure that contractually and ethically, you are able to do so.

Always, always remember to thank people. You may recall that George W. Bush's dad was also president. When he was in office, I think it was every weekend, he would hand-write thank you notes to key people in his life for the previous week, and just send these notes out to them. A hand-written thank you note from the leader of the western world. *That* is customer service.

You can do more. Contact the customer more frequently (remember what Vic Hunter said about the number of contacts required for customer retention, page 20), and give them legal gratuities. The gratuity level in government has a cap of $20 per gratuity, with nothing that can be converted to cash or has immediate cash value. You can offer white papers, books, and information. Again, I recommend the *Federal Personnel Guide*, which is published by Key Communications, as a superb gratuity, as it has extraordinary shelf life. And you can put a peel-and-stick label on it saying, "From your best friends at Amtower & Company. "

The *Guide* is a favorite of mine because it covers the mundane aspects of being a Federal employee: what happens at your next step increase, how to select the right health care provider or retirement plan during open season, how to prepare for a performance review, and other things those outside the government take for granted. Federal agencies do not make this information easily available for Federal employees. For that reason, the *Guide* has a longer shelf-life than you might expect. It also shows you care about the employee as an individual.

Other things you can do include special advance notice — first notice on pricing contracts, articles, etc. — invitations to events, and at events, special hospitality suites for your best customers, for your apostles and advocates.

Keep the MPC example in mind. They were at the 2003 FOSE, the large computer trade show here in Washington, D.C. for the federal government. They had a relatively modest exhibit space on the show floor itself, literally dwarfed by many other exhibits (see my perspective of trade shows in the Off-White Papers in Appendix 7). If you want my perspective of this FOSE, it is Off-White Paper 21, in the Appendix of this book. The exhibit hall was dominated by MicroWarehouse so getting mindshare was harder than usual. But off-site, the MPC hospitality suite had no such problem. Their absolute best customers, the customers from that limited number of agencies where they had significant mindshare, were treated extremely well, and properly thanked. Inside the hospitality suite, MPC did not allow sales material or sales people. They simply had food, drink, and executives to thank these people for being their best customers — well within ethical framework. And if they wanted to discuss certain products or services from MPC, they were escorted back across the street and introduced to their specific agency sales reps.

Ethical gratuities for federal employees could include, as previously mentioned, the *Federal Personnel Guide*. Remember the Vic Hunter contact model, and think of the number of times a federal employee may refer to the *Guide* during the course of a year, and seeing your company name and logo each time. If you want to test this concept, call Frank Joseph at (301) 656-0450. You can buy the *Federal Personnel Guide* in quantities as small as 40 (one case). If you order in large enough quantities, you can both customize the cover and replace the traditional 10 or so pages of advertising with your own advertising. The custom edition for PRC and the SuperMini contract was a big success.

Toys, tools, information, events — these are all valid things, as long as they stay within the ethical framework defined by the U.S. Office of Government Ethics, which you can find at www.usoge.gov.

Any giveaways you have should be quality items, preferably quality items with shelf life. I prefer quality items with shelf life and that have a response device, some way the buyer can contact you. Not simply your logo or your company name, but your web address or an 800 number. This allows them not only to remember you kindly, but to contact you as necessary. If you give away cheap stuff, you're sending a very unsubtle message that you really do not care about these people.

Examples of these would include:

- good pens (not cheap pens)

- post-it notes (not long shelf-life, but they would see your name each time they used a post-it)

- note pads and desk pads

- mouse pads (oldie but occasionally still a good one)

- pocket calendars (again, the nice ones that look like leather, not the real cheap ones)

- good coffee mugs and travel mugs

- portfolios

- canvas totes.

Keep in mind that all of your audiences include customers, press, vendor partners — anyone who likes your company (especially at the advocate and apostle levels) and who can positively influence others around them. This is anyone literally that you can develop a relationship with, including the press and vendors, as well as your customers.

And yes, you will occasionally come across the *"burn victim,"* the bottom side my pyramid, someone who is irate for real or imagined reasons. It doesn't really matter why they're angry. What matters is that you deal with this quickly.

Once you identify (or once they identify themselves to you) a burn victim, you have a senior manager address their concerns once they have identified themselves. Have the senior manager listen, act, do anything within reason ethically that they can, to placate this person. After they have taken care of the problem, have the same manager follow up again within two weeks while the issue is still burning inside that burn victim's mind.

If the issue has been resolved properly, what you will most likely do is convert the burn victim (the bottom of the pyramid) to an advocate or an apostle. This occurs because you have treated them the way that they want to be treated. You have treated them like the minor deity they perceive themselves to be.

The reason to deal with burn victims quickly and as completely as possible is that they talk about their experiences two-to-three times as much as advocates and apostles. A burn victim is the spoiler, and if they are people with influence, they can damage your chances in many ways.

These are not people you want running around hating you so loudly as to drown out all sane discussion. Each of us has been a burn victim somewhere along the line, and we each have our own stories — *which we will not forget*, and which we repeat with more frequency than you might imagine.

***

The last thing you can do — and this is very simple and relatively inexpensive — is to call or write customers just to say "thanks." Everyone likes and remembers special treatment, period. And sending even an e-mail, preferably a card, saying thank you is one way to do this. Not thank you and, by the way, we have a sale — *just thank you.*

I was on the board of FOSE, the trade show, from 1992 to 1994. We created a program where we identified and used our advocates, people who had attended the show, for the distribution of the invitations to the event. What we did was identify people who had attended the event for the last three years. Before we announced the dates publicly — it was known when the show was going to be — but before the public announcement, we would send these people an invitation saying, "Here is your free registration form for our upcoming conference and exposition, because we know you want to be here. And, by the way, if you would like to have some extra registration forms for your coworkers, please let us know how many." FOSE had some in-agency advocates back then — and this is well prior to e-mail distribution, mind you — and we had some people distributing up to three, four, five hundred in-agency registration forms for us just because we asked. This was an inexpensive and very effective program, and it *involved* the people that we wanted to involve in the event.

So, what are your action items for your customer relations programs? Think of your favorite places to shop (online or offline) and your favorite places to eat. What are the major features that make you want to go back?

What are you doing to identify your best buyers? And what are you doing to treat them well?

1 _____

2 _____

3 _____

4 _____

5 _____

CHAPTER FOUR

Public and Press Relations: Identifying and Creating Opportunities in the Press

The press brings a level of credibility that you cannot get through advertising, or in other venues. There is true power in the press: credibility. There is a certain amount of credibility bestowed upon anyone quoted in the press. Being written about, quoted or writing in the trade press is better advertising for you than many other things you do.

Do you ever wonder how some people and companies get more press than others? It does not come from prayer and fasting, or sending in enough box tops. It comes, in part, from *relationships* and hard work over time. Most importantly, it comes from having information that is newsworthy.

If you read the direct marketing press, you have probably seen my name many times, being quoted or writing stories for publications like *Catalog Age*, *Direct* and *DM News*. I am also in the federal trade press with some regularity, and have been quoted in Forbes twice. I work hard at press relations.

55

__Caveat:__ most companies should get professional advice on press relations, but like other outside services, this requires a company with strong contacts in the press community where you need exposure. If this is the Federal trade press, there are only a few companies and people who do this well, and __none__ of them are national PR firms.

To do this properly, you have to remember the first of the three questions: *what do you read?* You have to know which publications are most germane to your best customers, and which reporters are the most influential at those publications. Writers like Walter Mossberg (*Wall Street Journal*) and Stephen Wildstrom (*BusinessWeek*) have wide influence. A mention in a Mossberg column can sometimes bring venture capital into a company or cause a stock price to go up or down. Though they may not carry the same weight, there are probably editors and reporters who influence your niche. What are the three most influential publications in your niche?

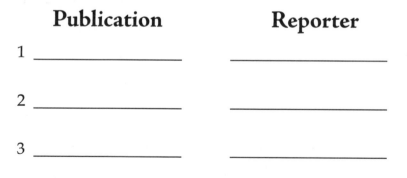

	Publication	**Reporter**
1	_____	_____
2	_____	_____
3	_____	_____

And who are the editors and reporters that most influence the readers? List these after each publication above.

All publication web sites have editorial calendars, reporter and editor contact information, and more. Many have the beat information, what each reporter or editor actually covers. They have notices on whether they accept outside submissions and there will be an explanation there as to what they look for. There will also be information on how to submit letters to the editor. And yes, there is visibility to be gained by "letters to the editor."

Each publication site has a search engine. Use the search engines to look for your company and see *who* wrote about you, look for your competitors and see *who* wrote about them, and determine from that which editors and reporters that you need to develop relationships with. Key people in your organization, *not just the PR staff* or outside PR firm, need to be tasked with contacting key reporters and editors responsible for your niche on a regular basis. Relationships must be developed.

There are reporters I speak with regularly, exchange e-mails with regularly, and one with whom I share a mutual love of diners, so we meet a couple times each year to eat at a local diner.

There are several issues to be addressed before speaking

with any member of the press. Your people also have to be properly coached on *how* to talk with the press. You have to have an explicit understanding with a reporter before you are truly on "background," and not offering quotable material. Do not assume all reporters and editors are of the same caliber. They are not.

You have to *know* key people at all publications. They have to be comfortable calling you. They have to know you well enough so that when you call them, they'll take your call. These are people that you inform first, regardless of whether or not it's good news. And when they call you, you have to be available, even if it's a no comment situation. You have to say, "Yes, something's going on, but I'm really not at liberty to comment on that at this time. " You develop trust over time, and it is a reciprocal trust.

So, what do you do for these relationships? You have to know which reporter owns which beat, and understand that this can and will change. Once you understand who covers what, you have to know what gets their attention. If you read some of their stories, you'll be able to determine what their hot buttons are. Is it controversy? Is it major dollars? Is it big names? You have to be able to determine what their hot buttons are if you are going to get their attention with your story.

I always send reporters kudos, even a quick e-mail

saying, "Great article." Not "Great article and why wasn't I mentioned?" It is similar to the way you should thank your best customers.

Most reporters are more used to getting grief from people, complaints about obvious omissions (why wasn't I called, or why wasn't my client mentioned). They aren't used to getting "thanks." If you have really neat toys, the same thing that you might send your best customer, send it to a reporter. If you've ever been to a reporter's cubicle, you will see that many of them have toys and giveaways from trade shows and other events that they have been to over the years. If you have something exceptional, send it to them, then follow up with a call. This is a good way to start a relationship.

To-Do List

Never, ever lie to or mislead a reporter. You don't get on the phone to them to bad-mouth, blame, to bitch, moan, groan— the BMG syndrome. You are there to share information with them, not to talk about, bad-mouth competitors or bad-mouth another reporter or publication.

If you are being interviewed, you might want to start the conversation with a predetermined list of things that *you* want to cover. Write these down beforehand. Make sure you mention each one a couple of times and check them off as you do so. When I know I am going to be interviewed on a specific topic, I write three things I want to emphasize on the big white board in my office, usually in the form of a short phrase. During the interview I will make certain to state each one three times, and put a check by the phrase each time I use it. This makes it more likely my words will make the story, not a paraphrase. This also increases the likelihood that one or more of my ideas will make it into the article.

Make your executives available to the reporters when they call. There will usually be some lead-time. Make sure your executives are capable of speaking in sound bites. Timing is everything.

Plan ahead: Calling after a special issue closes or is published is not going to help you at all. Look at the editorial calendars. Make sure you're in touch with the reporters and editors responsible for that editorial supplement or for that special issue well in advance of the publication date.

Hot topics and trends are always neat things for reporters to hear about, and controversy does sell.

Include all the publications that are pertinent to your company and niche. The most influential publication for your niche may not be a government trade publication. Almost all business and technical publications have some government subscribers and this may be the most critical audience for you to reach and influence. Government influencers read all manner of business publications, they attend all manner of business events, and they belong to all sorts of groups. So, if your cluster happens to be 200 people out of 50,000 readers, so be it. You still need to influence that publication. And it may be the publication you need to influence most frequently.

Over the years, I've gotten a number of tips from reporters on how to get their attention. The top one has always been, *"Build a relationship with me."* The reporters are looking for relationships with industry professionals. They rely on a network of these people for leads, quotes, confirmation and more.

Number two is *"the hook."* When you call them, lead with the hook. What is at stake in this story? Then, anticipate the "So what?" question: "What does this mean to our readers?" Make sure you have a good answer for that. Not just, "Well, because it's going to lead to the quarterly sales results that we want."

Then you must know what *that* reporter looks for: know what his hot buttons are. Understand what the publication covers, not just what you want it to cover. Know who the audience is for the publication. Get the BPA (Bureau of Publication Audit) statement and read it. Do not try to pitch a story that doesn't fit the publication. Find a publication where the story fits.

The biggest complaint I have seen from reporters is that some PR people (internal or external) pitch multiple reporters at one publication, or multiple reporters at several publications for a single story. If two reporters from competing publications show up with your story on the same day or the same week, you've just destroyed both relationships.

To develop a relationship, you contact a reporter to offer them an exclusive. Most of the reporters I have met over the years respect this, and they remember who provides the stories.

If you are asked by a competing reporter why they did not get the lead, you can tell the reporter that you will give them the story the next time — but only if you are really going to do it. If you sell the story to two reporters and they both cover it, you may look good briefly, but it's not likely that you have built any trust in that relationship. In all likelihood, you've burnt the bridge.

If you're a big enough and influential enough company, you might want to consider a private event for each trade publication in your niche once a year. Not an event where you invite all of the press, *but an event where you invite each publication separately*. Anytime you invite reporters or editors anywhere, feed them. Encourage them to stop by and visit when they're coming through your hometown or when they happen to be in the vicinity of your office.

Press relations could be the most single best investment in terms of impact. Being written about has serious impact and increases your credibility literally like nothing else out there.

Before we leave this, think about which trade publications you read (or should read). What attracts you to them?

What are your new action items for press? Who do you need to meet?

1 _____

2 _____

3 _____

4 _____

5 _____

CHAPTER FIVE

Events:
Selecting the right trade shows, boutique events, publication events, agency events, tabletop events that suit your niche

There is a simple fact of life in Washington, D.C. You can spend your professional life going from event to event, from 8:00 in the morning until early evening, virtually every workday of the week. You could spend your professional life out of the office going to events. I assume it is this way in other towns, but in Washington, these events center largely around the business of government.

Every single day, I find e-mails sent to me, or forwarded to me, about upcoming events. They are often sponsored by one of the publications, one of the research or consulting firms (Amtower & Company offers seminars on B2G marketing), or some out of the area company. Some have value, so do not.

Given that scenario, how do you determine where to spend your time, money and other resources? Again I refer you to the *Three Questions*, particularly question two: what do you attend? You cannot assume you know all the most important events for your niche. In some cases there are simply too many, making it hard to see which are truly valuable. You have to ask your best customers. Also, any industry event can and should be a networking event.

Here is a set of questions you should ask when deciding on event participation:

- what is the potential for return on investment?

- what else could you do with the money?

- what is the recent attendance history (up or down) ?

- will you be visible?

- are you reaching key audiences at this event?

- does this event draw from all CONUS (continental U.S.), or is it regional?

- is this an "ego" event?

- if you go, are you exploiting the right opportunities?

Then comes the money question. What should I pay to exhibit or otherwise participate? Major events, big trade shows, eat major dollars. There's no way to get around this. FOSE costs about $50 per foot for floor space on the exhibit hall. Attendance is down at many of the larger events. eGov folded as a stand-alone event. COMDEX declared bankruptcy, and cancelled the event for 2004 (we have yet to see if they will actually return). They say they will re-emerge in 2005. It's not a government event, but it had always been a major IT industry event.

If you're going to go to major event (read: expensive), will you be visible, and how will you be visible? What is the return versus the other activities that you might be able to fund with this same money? Are you reaching key audience by attending this major event? Does the event draw from all of the continental U.S.?

Is this an ego event? Did somebody sell a concept to your executives or you that if you're not here, you're not a player?

And if you go, are you exploiting all of the available opportunities that this brings to the table?

The event to-do checklist:

- pre-show, at show, post-show communication

- booth personnel training

- have something special for your current best customers

- hold press and customer briefings

- host a hospitality suite

- speaking opportunities

- other?

At the Federal Business Council site, you can download a good *Exhibitor Planning Guide* (www.fbcinc.com/resources.asp).

Getting Your Bang for the Buck from Trade Shows

From my point of view, it's difficult to get bang for the buck out of any big trade show. It does not occur by relying exclusively on floor traffic at your booth, as many seem to hope.

There are many ways to enhance your presence, but where is, and how do you measure, the return on your investment?

There is the booth space, the show guide, the event web site, on-site meeting rooms, speaking opportunities, pre-show and post-show marketing opportunities. You can negotiate and brainstorm with the trade show staff to make certain that you get the most bang for your buck. One Amtower & Company client finds that a more modest presence on the showroom floor, not the biggest — which they could afford — booth on the floor, is offset by having meeting rooms where they take customers for educational opportunities. This company also hosts lunches in its meeting rooms.

For "meet and greet" opportunities, food is important. Never host any event over an hour without some kind of food. For a lunch, having a really top-notch speaker could be good. If the speaker goes over well, it won't matter whether or not they are from the government market. If the speaker flops, the same holds true.

Meeting rooms work for many companies at trade shows, often much better than having the largest booth on the floor. There is much less distraction and *you* get to control the environment. As long as you attract the right audience, this is something you should consider.

The Ego Issue

Over the years I have heard the argument that if you are not at (fill in the name of a big event), you are not a player. The idea that you're a player in the market only if you show up at any event, just isn't accurate. Major companies, including Dell, have continually reevaluated their presence at federal trade shows and chosen to be minimally represented. Several years back, Compaq, when it was a stand-alone, pulled out of a major Federal event. They saved $300,000, total dollars spent, including booth, drayage, personnel time and all that, and they spent the money in different marketing programs and actually grew their marketshare as a result. So the argument that if you're not there, you're not a player just doesn't have any validity.

In recent years, visual domination of major events has become more popular. Examples of this include the big, colorful bags on the show floor, aisle signage, and big banners at the entryways. In my opinion, trade show visual domination has little long-term impact. If you exhibit, there are other ways to maximize the value.

Niche Events.

Niche events fall into several categories. They can be technical, agency specific, in-agency table-tops, information/

educational from specific vendors, association or special interest group events, for small business, for large contractors, excuses for getting together for dinner and drinks, or true value-adds for the attendees. They vary in length of time from an hour or two to multiple days.

Given that there are so many events offered by companies new to the market, the first thing to do is check the pedigree. Find event producers with a track record in this market, who you heard about from customers or people in the market you respect. Do not assume, as many do, that a well-written e-mail from a company you never heard of will provide a venue of significance. It rarely happens.

Some of the better providers are the Federal Business Council (www.fbcinc.com), the Digital Government Institute (www.digitalgovernmetn.com), the Immix Group (**www. immixgroup.com**)—which offers very good sales seminars, and OCI (good proposal training, www.orgcom.com). Several companies offer breakfast briefings and seminars: Federal Sources (www.fedsources.com) , Input (www.input.com), ENC Marketing (www.encmarketing.com), CMA (www.cmai.com) and others. Networking is just as important as the information you get at some of these, and often it is more important.

Many of the premier networking and educational events are provided by the special interest groups and associations. AFCEA (www.afcea.org) has events all over the country. The ones in the D.C. area are exceptional networking opportunities. The American Council for Technology (ACT, formerly FGIPC, www.fgipc.org) and its affiliates, especially the Industry Advisory Council (IAC, www.iaconline.org), are critical for any company selling information technology. IAC has a Western Council based in Denver that is also quite active. The monthly AFFIRM luncheon (www.affirm.org) has been a great networking venue for years.

There are several other excellent groups and forums, and there are pretenders. Check for the pedigree. A new event hosted by a company that has been in the market could be worthwhile, but a new event hosted by a company new to the market is wishful thinking.

I find the smaller events, especially the in-agency events, where the event occurs inside a government agency, to be of more tactical value, often with more immediate return on your investment, both return on the dollar investment and return on your time investment.

You only have a limited amount of time to do events, and a lot of the tabletop events, the niche events, are half-day events, with little drayage or the other logistics of a large event. You go in, you have a tabletop there, you have a little pop-up display, you hand out your materials, you get to talk to real people, usually inside of real agencies. Federal Business Council (fbcinc.com) is a wonderful provider of these type of events. They do over 150 a year. FBC is also doing more single agency, multi-day events. The Digital Government Institute (www.digitalgovernment.com) hosts high-end IT seminars and workshops, usually two-day events on very specific topics like enterprise, architecture, or web security, those types of things. One way to check pedigree is to look at a producer's web site. If you do this with the Digital Government Institute, and look at the Advisory Board, you will see instant pedigree.

Federal agencies themselves host events, oftentimes using companies like the Federal Business Council for the logistics side. But it is the agency itself hosting the event and the agency guaranteeing a certain level and number of attendees. There are publication-hosted events, association chapter events, and special interest group events.

These niche events always require less time, money, and effort. They can put you in front of a key audience *if* you're very selective about how you choose these events. You also have to respond early, as there is limited exhibit space at these events.

That being said, beware of *black hole events*. Since 9/11, a number of black hole events have emerged.

What are black hole events? These are would-be events from producers who are here for a quick buck. They have no pedigree, and not much in the way of industry depth or breadth, ensuring there will be little of consequence discussed and few of importance with whom to network.

There has been tons of e-mail and snail mail from these would-be event producers, touting the fee-based access to agency CIOs, or perhaps budget information that you're not going to get elsewhere. Most of the companies producing these would-be events have no track record in this market, and they have no relationships with real players in this market. What they will deliver will be minimal at best, and it will cost you a lot of money. Ask them what the value is to this event, where is their track record, who attended or exhibited last year? Ask how long they've been doing this in the government market and who on their staff is known in this market? Another way to ask this is, what is your bandwidth? How many people attended this event last year and the year before? Can I get some references from past attendees or exhibitors? Can I see the registration list from previous years? Who are your sponsors? Can I call them? Who is your contact in sponsoring organizations and who were your sponsors last year? And, is the agenda set? By this, I mean are the invited speakers actually confirmed, or have they even acknowledged the receipt of an invitation? We have all seen the announcements with "invited" speakers. On many occasions when I have contacted the "invited" speakers, they are not aware of the event or their "participation."

If the producers of these events who are trying to sell you exhibit space or sponsorships dance around any of the above questions, you know you're dealing with a provider of a nonexistent event. Hang up the phone, then spray it with Lysol.

Speaking at events can raise your overall credibility in the market. Like being quoted or written about in the publications, speaking at an event is a significant indicator that you (your company) are a player in the market. Usually this will require exhibiting at an event. On the conference side of some events, that's not always true. On the keynote side, it almost always is. You have to develop and pursue these opportunities Usually the lead time to get a keynote is over a year, unless your company or company spokesperson is hot. Keynotes can lend extraordinary credibility to your efforts.

However, it is important to make certain that whoever is going out there to speak on behalf of your company *is well trained to do so*. The credibility that speaking at an event affords you can evaporate very quickly if you send someone out there who is not a good public speaker, who is not a good public presence for your company. I have had clients swear to me that their CEO was a great speaker, only to have it turn out that the CEO was marginal at best. A poorly delivered keynote, or a keynote not germane to the audience, can do serious damage to your company and its present and future marketing efforts.

Once you decide where you will sponsor and exhibit, you can publicize your participation in events through the "events" page at your web site. If you don't have one yet, this is a method to keep your web site more informationally robust. You can also publicize events in your own e-newsletter, and in your space ads. In early 2004, PC Mall put a small banner across their space ads that read, "See us at FOSE." You can promote this with targeted direct mail. Your inside and outside sales staff should have a regular updated list of the events where you will be, and they should be telling all of their customers, regionally and nationally, where you will be. If you use one of those call-waiting messages—and I hope you do not—use it well. This is the type of information that could work on a call-waiting message, as long as you change your message regularly.

For event selection and marketing, what are your new action items?

1 _____

2 _____

3 _____

4 _____

5 _____

CHAPTER SIX

Direct Marketing to the Feds

Direct marketing is any one-to-one correspondence with customer or prospect — snail mail, e-mail, or even fax. During the dot-com era, many were fond of saying "direct mail (snail mail) is dead!" It just isn't so — and it never was. Snail mail has always been a prime way to reach prospects and stay in touch with your key government contacts.

Has e-mail changed snail mail? Maybe, but as long as we have thumbs, snail mail will live.

What are the benefits of B2G direct marketing (snail and e-mail)? You can have targeted messages to very defined audiences. It is *off the radar* of your competitors (e-mails are easily forwarded, snail mail is not). It can be executed quickly to take advantage of the changing landscape, particularly in the e-communications mode, and it allows you to deliver different messages to different audiences.

A high level executive is not going to need to know all of the technical differentiators of a product. A procurement

79

office only needs to know the product, source, price, and terms, where they can buy it. They don't need to know the technical information. The user needs to know the technical information.

B2G direct mail (again, snail and e-mail) tips include:

- Good **list selection**, know the source, trust the source.

- Use **only your company logo on the envelope**, on the carrier. Do not load up, as most ad agencies would have you do, with teaser copy and other things that will show that this is, in government parlance, unsolicited commercial mail.

- Use the mail to **drive** them to your 800 number and the web.

- Give them **multiple reasons** to get in touch with you, and test the response devices that you're going to use prior to getting that mail out.

- Catalogs should be in **envelopes**. We've seen a number of tests over the years, particularly in DoD and military base situations where catalogs in mail have a much higher response rate than catalogs as self-mailers.

- **Avoid over-mailing the DoD** and military facilities. We know that there are thresholds beyond which mail is not delivered. The original published statements were for the Air Force, 50 pieces of mail, delivered on the same or consecutive days by the same identifiable mailer need not be delivered. We believe the threshold is about 25 now, and it applies to all military base activities.

- Clearly **state the contracts** the product or service is available on—where they can buy it, how they can buy it.

- And use the **SmartPay logo** on all correspondence. The government credit card is largely used for micro-purchase, purchases under $2,500. But roughly five percent of the cards issued—and there are over 300,000 cards used at the federal level for purchasing—have a warrant level. And this means that on a per purchase basis, they can go anywhere from $2,501 up to and including low six-figure purchases. Some cards out there are capable of doing a six- or seven-figure purchase on a single transaction. *Use the SmartPay logo.*

Snail mail still works. Government employees (especially those who are supervisors and managers) receive lots of mail and respond to that which is germane to them. Lots of this mail is delivered to employees in Washington, D.C., where the anthrax issue and mail delays still occur.

In D.C., our studies indicate that senior executives—all

agencies in D.C. — receive mail three times a day, usually mid-morning, around lunchtime, and the early-to-mid afternoon. There are three deliveries each day, with senior executives receiving up to 25 to 30 pieces per delivery. Having watched these people open their mail, I can tell you that they spend roughly 10 to 15 seconds with each piece max before they decide whether to save it to read later, to route it to their staff, or to throw it away. A lot of mail is actually routed to staff, as long as it is germane to their needs. According to Market Connections, three main reasons the Feds look at mail are

- *it's from a known vendor*

- *it is germane to the current needs*

- *the staff might need this.*

List sources

The government **publication lists** are usually the best. However, keep in mind that publications in general, not just the government publications, all have clusters of government readers, so it may be a non-government publication that will provide you your best government leads. Remember the Three Questions: what do you read?

Response lists, attendees, buyers, inquirers, lists of people who have attended, inquired, or purchased, people who have responded to anything. These are people who obviously respond to offers of some kind.

There are a variety of **compiled lists,** but the bottom line here is to know the source. Don't buy lists because you received some e-mail saying, "We have a hundred thousand government buyers available on a CD-ROM for fifty bucks." Blue sky is blue sky. Know the source. The Amtower & Company list of GSA SmartPay cardholders is available through Merit Direct (www. MeritDirect.com). Amtower & Company has been compiling government lists since 1985.

There are a variety of publications that serve the government market: *American City and County, Federal Computer Week, Governing Magazine, Government Computer News, Government Executive, Government Product News, Government Procurement, Government Technology, Government Video. Washington Technology* serves the systems integrators in contractor community.

There are the general business publications that have those targeted clusters of government buyers, and these could provide you your best prospects. If a publication regularly shows up in your surveys of your best customers, look carefully at that publication. Get the publication audit statement; take a close look at the web site. This could be the place where you need to develop a deeper relationship with the publication.

I will be dealing with this—I call it a one-book buy—a little later on.

Different mail packages for different audiences

End-users need a performance message, ease of use, the *BFEC*—the better, faster, easier, cheaper information.

Decision-makers, the bosses, need productivity. How is this going to make my staff more productive?

Procurement offices need price, source, terms, business status—are you a small business, large business—and what types of contracts your products are available on, if any.

Use mail to support space ad campaigns, events, and especially end of fiscal year in the government market.

The packages that seem to work best are catalogs, number 10 packages (your standard letter size), and postcards work, particularly outside of D.C. Inserts in publications are also good.

In envelopes, avoid the Ed McMahon syndrome. You remember when Ed McMahon was on the envelope from American Family Publishers and when you opened the envelope, there were about 10 to 15 different items in there. It was confusing and very time-consuming.

Government employees do not have this type of time, and

you do not need to test their patience. Your message has to be clear, succinct, and immediate. Ten to 15 seconds is all they'll spend with this mail piece. If you confuse them, they will trash it.

The Message

If you have a limited time, define and emphasize your differentiators. Do you accept credit cards? Do you have a variety of contracts? Do you have specific contracts that you're pushing with this particular mail piece? Is this an awareness piece, announcing a new company or product?

Your differentiators can include:

- are you **small** business, minority 8a, woman-owned, veteran-owned, a hub zone?

- Do you have a large **contract selection**?

- Are you pushing a **single contract**?

- Do you have a lot of **government experience**? Government buyers like to know that your company has done business with the government before, and preferably for a long time.

- Has your company been **in business a long time**? The longevity of your business.

- Can you **deliver** product faster?

- Do you have a **broad range of products**? Or are you more of a niche product or service?

Response devices

It has to be as easy as possible for people to respond and order from you. And don't predicate this on what *you* think; test the response devices. Fax is less important these days, but occasionally it is still used, so you have to keep it in the mix for the time being. An 800 number should go directly to an order desk. Mail options should include a prepaid envelope or postcard for order forms. If you ask for an e-mail address, always ask for the opt-in. Tell them you're going to use the e-mail to correspond with them regularly, but you will not let other people use the e-mail. Your web response devices have to be tracked and tested on a regular basis.

When to mail

End of the government fiscal year (FY) is the most important time to be in front of customer, and I define end of FY as any time in the May through September time frame. The official end of FY is September 30. You have to be in front of that audience on a regular basis through the end of FY to remind them that you're there.

This is not the best time for prospecting. If you have a lot of money, you can prospect. *It is the best time to be in front of customers who already buy from you.* October 1st, the beginning of the government's FY, is the next spike and a good time to mail if there's not a continuing resolution, i.e., if the budgets have been approved. November, December, January is pretty slow. Business begins to pick up around mid-January. March and April shows the beginning of SmartPay, the credit card increase in spending. And mailing before and after events is always important.

Problem areas

The military base activities restrict the number of pieces arriving. The Social Security Administration is the only federal agency I know of in 20 years of doing this that requires first class delivery, and that is to a single zip code, 21235. The reason is simple. They spend a lot of time making certain that their constituent mail, mail from old people with perhaps less than great hand-writing, gets to the right office. Security agencies do not deliver commercial mail; forget it. You need the relationships in there, anyway. And consider using the publications as your best delivery vehicles. We will talk about this when I go to the one-book buy.

E-mail to government is working, but what was three years ago a very high response rate is dropping. And it's those who aren't responding to your e-mails that you should worry most about.

The federal webmasters have been very proactive in sharing information on spam and other web-related items for several years now. And they've had guidelines out for several years. They've shared their best practices for several years. What is news on the business-to-consumer and business-to-business front on spam legislation and all this, is old news in the government market. The spam barriers, things like surf control, have been up for years. And ISPs designated as spammers are not getting through at all. If you use e-mail as a primary communication tool, develop a suppression file. For those people who contact you and who do not want e-mail, put them on your suppression file and any time your company is going to do an e-mail campaign, make sure you use the suppression file to take the people off who do not want the information.

Amtower's Fifth Law: Spam is good for toast.

There is no other way to say this. If you use spam and you've developed a wonderful rapport with all these people, built great relationships, got credibility in the press, got all the events properly, all of that stuff, you could kill it by spamming people. Everybody hates spam, and some people are very active about it (remember *burn victims*).

Spam is good for toast.

Intelligent e-marketing, on the other hand, is not that difficult, but it is a very incremental process. Limit the size of your e-mail and don't use attachments. Both e-mail size and attachments are triggers for spam filters. Sponsor other newsletters, the trade publications, the associations, the special interest groups all have e-communications and many of them sell sponsorships or advertisements inside those e-newsletters. If you're going to use e-mail, put the opt-out at the top, not at the bottom. Strongly encourage pass-along readership, "Send this to your friends"… "Please forward."

Develop your own opt-in newsletter. This is going to be a very slow process, and it can be discouraging. But if you do it right—the way, perhaps ASAP.com had done it, or some of the other vendors—then you will see an incremental build-up in the traffic and encourage your best customers to go there and to sign up. But when you do this, make sure you tell them that you are not going to allow third party participation, i.e., you will not rent the list or give it to other people for use. It's for your use only. You have to be CAN-SPAM compliant. If you have any questions about that, go to the Direct Marketing

Association (www.the-dma.org) and look for the CAN-SPAM rules.

When you develop your opt-in newsletter, it should include specials with direct links to those specials, upcoming events with direct links at your site to those events. Have real news, with direct links to those stories. The reason for direct links is to take them directly to the part of your site they are interested in. Do not take them to the homepage and assume that they can find their way around your web site. Your newsletter should take them directly to the portions of the web site that they want to get to. Keep it simple.

Test advertising in the other e-newsletters, e-pubs, *Federal Computer Week, Government Computer New, Government Executive Magazine.* There are many association newsletters out there, as well as special interest groups. If you need to reach contractors, try *Washington Technology* (www.WashingtonTechnology.com) or *Government Express* (www.GovernmentExpress.com).

Try to get placement in government *list serves.* We know, for instance, that the Federal Communicators Network, a special interest group inside the government responsible for dissemination of information inside their respective agencies, share event information through their list serve. We have seen many events promoted by them to their agencies over the years.

We have seen e-mail used to announce the arrival of potentially incoming snail mail, especially catalogs. We have seen regular specials for best customers announced via e-mail. We've seen e-announcements swapped with channel partners, or resellers swapping with manufacturers. And we've seen e-mail and snail mail used for reorder reminders. A thank you note that says, "A couple months ago, you ordered XYZ from us; according to our records, you order regularly enough that this is probably something you need to reorder at this time."

Need an example of a really good e-mail? Here's one, courtesy of the Digital Government Institute:

> From: **Digital Government Institute**
> **<phelan1@comcast.net>**
> To: <amtower@erols.com>
> Subject: **Agency Web Content Mgt Solutions Dec 8-9**
> Date: Tue, 19 Oct 2004 07:57:22 -0600 (MDT)

```
* * * * * * * * * * * * * * * * * * * * * * * * * * * * * * * * * * * * * * * * * * * * * *

19-Oct-04

* * * * * * * * * * * * * * * * * * * * * * * * * * * * * * * * * * * * * * * * * * * * *

This newsletter contains:

1.

* * * * * * * * * * * * * * * * * * * * * * * * * * * * * * * * * * * * * * * * * * * * *

WEB CONTENT MANAGEMENT CLINIC

December 8-9, 2004
```

George Washington University, Washington, D.C.
(Foggy Bottom Metro Stop)

Learn how to:

* Develop an agency Web Content Management Roadmap

* Evaluate Content Management Software Vendors

* Design Effective Web Publishing Processes and Workflow

* Analyze your site's content to develop a taxonomy and metadata standards.

Spend 2 days with faculty Tony Byrne (Founder and Editor, CMS Watch) and Lisa Welchman (Principal, Welchman Consulting), and web content management implementers across the federal government, as they teach you how to resolve your federal agency web content management issues. You will receive practical instruction, as well as realistic guidance and lessons learned from government practitioners.

Leave the seminar with a checklist of your organizational web content management concerns and next steps for creating CM solutions within your own organization.

PLUS

"60 Seconds with a CMS Vendor," moderated by Tony Byrne. Bring your candid questions and receive candid answers from content management software vendors.

Presenting Organizations
Digital Government Institute
Welchman Consulting

Council for Excellence in Government
GSA
George Washington University

Media Sponsor - CMS Watch

Planning Committee
Dana Hallman, Office of the Controller of the
Currency, Treasury Department
Sanjay Koyani, Dept. of Health and Human Services
Renee Lockhardt Trujillo, Social Security
Administration
Gina Pearson, Agency Web Manager, Economic Research
Service, USDA
Lisa Welchman, Welchman Consulting

4 Easy Ways to Register:
Online: www.digitalgovernment.com
By Phone: 202-624-1762
By Fax: 202-624-1766
By Mail: DGI c/o Meeting Management Services (MMS),
1201 New Jersey Ave., NW,
Washington, D.C. 20001

Registration Fee:
$795 - Government, with payment by credit card or
check in advance
$995 - Industry, with payment by credit card or
check in advance

Group discounts available.

Digital Government Institute, LLC, 6213 Crathie
Lane, Bethesda, MD 20816

```
Click here for program details and to register.

http://www.mymailout.com/mymailout/do/article/view?
id=35603&lm=1150356

* * * * * * * * * * * * * * * * * * * * * * * * * * * * * * * * * * * * * * * * * * * * * * * * * * * * * *

Visit http://www.digitalgovernment.com

* * * * * * * * * * * * * * * * * * * * * * * * * * * * * * * * * * * * * * * * * * * * * * * * * * * * * *

To subscribe or unsubscribe:

http://www.mymailout.com/mymailout/subscribe/
?listid=1183&runid=11596
```

This e-mail is short, informative, and has enough information without having too much. It has the agenda, the fee, what you can expect to learn, the value-add "Plus," and four ways to register (make it easy). One other item that shows this is a worthwhile event is the "Planning Committee" list of advisors, the kind of people you hope to see at an event like this, whether you are government or industry . The only mistake I find is that there is not a direct link to the event part of the web page—just a link to the Digital Government web site. Once there, the event is easy to find, though.

So, what are your action items for your direct, snail, or e-communications programs?

1 _____

2 _____

3 _____

4 _____

5 _____

CHAPTER SEVEN

Space Advertising

I will offer only a few observations on space advertising, starting with space advertising (like major trade shows) can be an expensive proposition. But, it is not a one-time, once-a-year deal like trade shows. Space advertising cannot be a one-time occurrence if it is to be successful.

Space advertising is a repetitious activity if you are going to get any traction out of it at all. But, more importantly, what do the space ads require to be effective?

In the government market, we have seen a lot of glitz and a lot of tremendously dull things. What seems to work are the duller items — contract information, product information, pricing, and response mechanisms, the web address, new product information. It has to be informational while catching the eye. Take a look at the Dell ads. You will see three major things over and over again: product, price, and source. And Dell has been doing it for years and the ads have been very successful.

The glitzier the advertisement is, the more potentially confusing it might be. Space advertising is very good for branding and possibly for positioning, but it's extremely public, and by that I mean it's on everybody's radar. Absolutely everybody in the universe knows what you are doing, unlike direct mail or e-mail. The glitzier your ad, the more likely it is that you will have what I call the "Herschel" factor. Hershel Gordon Lewis is a curmudgeon who writes for one of the marketing publications. He did a keynote speech that I saw once called, "The 'Huh?' Factor." Any advertisement that makes you go, "Huh?" is one that you are likely to pass over, i.e., continue flipping the pages of a magazine and not go back to that ad. There have been several of these along the way over the years, and you do not want to be part of this syndrome.

Dell does not exhibit that syndrome. Product, price, source, very dull. MPC, product, price, source; CDW-G—product, price, source. Possibly dull, but very effective. Go with what's effective. *You are not here to be subservient to an ad agency.* The ad agency is going to try to sell you glitz. It doesn't work in this market, and I don't care if it works somewhere else. It might work in Hollywood where they think $5 billion is big money.

Space ads in nontraditional government publications, the ones your best customers tell you they're reading, could be very important. The way to government-ize those advertisements, very simply, is to put the GSA logo or the SmartPay logo in a corner of the advertisement. Government buyers will know what this means; they'll recognize it for what it is, and it will not detract from the advertisement for the other readers of that publication. Again, don't let your ad agency dictate what goes in the advertisement. Very few ad agencies understand *anything* about the government market, yet they attempt to control your ad spending in every market.

For any publication ad, it's important to get (and read) the Bureau of Publication Audit (BPA) statement from the publication itself. This will segment who the readers are by industry, by their job functional area. Read this carefully and make the determination if this is really where you want to spend your money.

Avoid publications that are not audited. The coffee table tomes, the start-up publications from companies like those who are producing the nebulous events — these are companies with little or no government experience who are here simply in the post-9/11 environment because all of a sudden, they know that there are billions and billions of dollars being spent, and they want your money. (See the Off-White Papers on publications in the Appendix). If they're not audited, they're not worth it.

Space ads are not one-time deals; they have to be part of an ongoing campaign. It may be part of the space campaign.

It may be part of a campaign for a specific time of year, so one, two, or three ads might work for you, as long as it's in conjunction with an event, with a snail mail campaign, with an e-mail campaign, or a variety of other components coming together.

The One-Book Buy

Let's talk briefly about those one-book buys that I've been mentioning. If a publication continuously shows up in your surveys of your best customers—it has a mailing list, it has a web site, it probably has an e-newsletter, it might produce events. It has inserts and advertising, it has multiple opportunities for you to maximize the dollar value of your relationship with the publication. And if you approach any of these publications with the idea that you're going to spend more money with them, they will become extremely creative in working with you to maximize your spending of money with them, but to maximize your exposure through their various media. This is to their benefit because it means that you will be getting bang for the buck as long as they deliver, and it's less likely that somebody will be able to wean you away from them as long as they keep producing with and for you. It also allows you to negotiate and get better prices for each of the components that you might be using.

What do space ads need?

- *product or service information*

- *contract information*

- *pricing*

- *web address*

- *multiple response devices*

- *and it should be informational while catching the eye.*

So, what is your action list for space advertising?

1 _____

2 _____

3 _____

4 _____

5 _____

CHAPTER EIGHT

Special Interest Groups and Associations

In my 20 years experience in the government market, I have found that there are special interest groups (SIGs) for virtually every niche where I have done research. It doesn't really matter how seemingly mundane—facility management, mail management, hundreds of different information technology components—there are special interest groups out there for everything.

Many associations, national professional associations, have government chapters. There are national professional groups, special interest groups on a formal or informal basis. There are inter- and intra-agency groups. There is a Pentagon Mac users group, for instance.

Even though they don't rank tremendously high in the Market Connections study, SIGs often represent some extremely powerful niches. And when you identify the right ones, you are real close to being at the focal point of your niche universe. If you identify the right special interest groups, this can give you extraordinary face time with a very, very targeted audience. So, remember the "R" word, relationships, and Question Three— *What do you belong to?*

A good example of a special interest group is the Senior Executive Association. Remember, there are only about 6,000 career Senior Executive Service members in the government. At last count, the Senior Executive Association represented about 4,000 of them. If you need to reach the top personnel people in government at the Assistant Secretary or that level, the InterAgency Group (IAG) is the place to be.

The Armed Forces Communication and Electronics Association (AFCEA) is a national organization and has chapters literally all over the world. Rational Software, now owned by IBM, has a federal users group. SIGCAT, the Special Interest Group for CD-ROM Applications and Technology, (now part of the DVD Association of America) is still associated with what used to be called FGIPC, the Federation of Government of Information Processing Councils, now known as ACT, American Council for Technology. The Joint Financial Management Improvement Program, roughly 800 individuals, has been around for probably 20 or 25 years now and represents the top bean counters — accounting, accounting technology professionals, and budgetary people inside government.

I mentioned the Federal Communicators Network earlier. These are people responsible inside each agency for the dissemination of information inside their agencies, and they have a great list serve. You want to get esoteric, try the Interagency Motor Equipment Advisory Council, IMEAC. IMEAC has less than a thousand members, but these are the people responsible for the largest land fleets, sea fleets, and air fleets in the world. The Association for Federal Information Resource Management (AFFIRM) is a place where I met several key people 20 years ago. Many of these people are still active have evolved into key people at this stage of the game, and they're still involved in AFFIRM. The Industry Advisory Council, known as the IAC (pronounced EYE-ack) inside the beltway in Washington, is the group of the top 400 information technology contractors. About 95 percent of all government IT contracts are owned by members of the IAC. If you need to develop relationships with the systems integrator community, there is no place better than the IAC.

WITC, the Western Information Tech Council, has an IAC chapter out in Denver, but WITC itself is comprised of federal, regional IT CIO type level people, as well as 13 western state CIOs. As of this writing, the Denver-based IAC has Jim Ridgell, who founded the original IAC in D.C., and he is still a heck of a guy.

If you need to know about mail, the Committee on Mail Policy in the federal government is still an active group.

As an active SIG, special interest group participant, you're demonstrating your unselfish desire to help people in an area where they are sharing information amongst themselves. You do not send your most aggressive sales people to be participants, to be members of the special interest group. You send your most knowledgeable, helpful people to participate. This should allow you to develop those long-term relationships you really need to maximize your presence in this market.

This market is built on relationships. If you are willing to put in the time and effort, find the right SIGs, you can make a great living.

You should have active members at all pertinent special interest groups and associations targeting your niche and a method internally at your organization for sharing what each of these special interest groups or associations is up to, so you can determine what type of monetary commitment to make to each. Do you need to sponsor an upcoming conference? Do you need to sponsor a luncheon? Will it have the right people there? Is the agency that you're most interested in growing mindshare and going to be a significant participant at an upcoming SIG luncheon? It would behoove you to sponsor that luncheon.

A lot of the special interest groups host events beyond simply monthly luncheons. The DVD-SIGCAT group hosts conferences annually. Exhibit space at the conference is $1,200. Every other year the Department of Interior facility managers host a Facilities Management Conference, roughly a thousand people, and they invite other agency facility managers to be there. The exhibit cost in 2004 — and this is an every other year event — was $850. It puts you in front of a significant audience at an extremely low cost.

The Interagency Motor Equipment Advisory Council, IMEAC, had its last conference in June 2003, with 800 or so key Motor Equipment Advisory members, the people responsible for those huge fleets and huge budgets. Exhibiting was $1,200.

How are you identifying the special interest groups? How are you getting in front of them? What are your action items for this audience?

1 _____

2 _____

3 _____

4 _____

5 _____

CHAPTER NINE

End of FY Tactics

End of FY Marketing Tips

(These were compiled from a presentation at the 2004 Federal Channels: panel included Lisa Dezzutti of Market Connections, David Powell of the Federal Business Council, and Mark Amtower)

1. Know your customer—ask the right questions.
   a. What do you read; what do you attend; what do you belong to
   b. Know what they want to buy, who they're currently buying from, when and how
   c. Ask, listen, act

2. Monitor competitors closely during end-of-FY
   a. How does the market perceive you relative to them?
   b. Emphasize what makes you different

3. Clearly emphasize and communicate your differentiators during end of FY—service, delivery, 8(a), woman-owned, 24 hour ordering, etc.

4. Integrate your End of FY campaigns
   a. Consistent look and message
   b. What's in their hand must resonate with what they see on the web

5. Use multiple tactics
   a. Direct mail, web, PR, telemarketing, events
   b. No one shot campaigns without a supporting cast

6. Use space ads selectively, make them direct response ads—awareness-building should be done earlier in the year.

7. Consider the One-Book Buys for space ads.

8. Exploit best accounts (agency accounts): if an agency likes you, spend more time/money there (all locations) than elsewhere; table tops, direct mail, e-mail.

9. Mail to your installed customer base every other week July/August—every week in Sept: snail and e-mail.

10. Use the same list three times for prospecting.

11. If you go after low-hanging fruit (sales under $2,500), mail the credit card file 2x (outside D.C.) in August/Sept

12. Send all mail in D.C. area in envelopes; remember all D.C. snail mail is still irradiated.

13. Post cards work outside D.C., but not at base activities.

14. Make your messages matter
    a. Must have stopping power—relevant headlines and short copy
    b. Consistency and frequency

15. Include information to help make decisions
    a. Prices, specs
    b. Web site address/800 number
    c. Contract vehicles

16. Include a government theme—let them know you understand their business.

17. Give multiple ways to respond—web, phone, fax, BRC.

18. Follow-up on all leads...70% are not followed up on.

19. Give multiple ways to buy
    a. Online with a credit card

b. Multiple contracts

20. Establish year-end blanket purchase agreements—easy way to buy.

21. Weekly spot reductions from your GSA Schedule price through busy season.

22. Leverage legal gratuities. Include Federal Personnel Guide with every Sept sale—call 301-656-0450 and tell Frank Joseph that Mark Amtower sent you—announce this at your web site.

23. E-mails should lead with end-of-FY special and gratuity offer.

24. Extend business hours and communicate it!

25. Answer the phone.

26. Guarantee calls returned within one hour.

27. Put specials on your hold music, tell about extended hours.

28. Use SmartPay logo on all promo material.

29. Make your web site uscr friendly
    a. Loads quickly
    b. Easy to navigate
    c. Content rich

30. Keep the web site fresh—update weekly through busy season: specials, news, links.

31. Leverage testimonials or other success stories.

32. Create white papers that can be posted on web site for downloading, used as leave-behinds on account calls and used as response incentive in direct marketing efforts.

33. Telemarketing to existing accounts with end of year specials.

34. Have sales contests in your outbound office.

35. Maximize linkage July-October; links with publications, manufacturer partners, channel partners, FBC, GovFacility—wherever you can get links at sites that get the right traffic.

36. Call your sales rep at the publication that works best for you and ask them for the best they can do between now & Oct 15.

37. Plan press releases for busy season…work to get editorial coverage.

38. Meet a new reporter—one whose beat covers your niche; there may be no immediate payoff, but who knows…

39. Ask customers for referrals.

40. Reward frequent buyers—always say thank you.

41. Customer appreciation days—special delivery packages— cookies, etc.

42. Hand out ice cream at key agencies one afternoon a week.

43. Have executive team distribute busy season survival kits.

44. Sales blitz days—close order and pick up purchase order, etc., make it a contest, take execs with you.

45. Special events—seminars—face-to-face marketing.

46. Participate in more in-agency events until November.

47. Have execs speak at events and SIG meetings.

48. Be visible at SIG meetings. Attend AFFIRM, PKI, FISSEA & others where there will be a concentration of Feds.

49. If you are known in a niche look for affinity groups in government with list serves; see if they will carry your end-of-FY message: FISSEA, GCN, PKI, etc.

50. Sponsor events/breakfasts and network at these meetings.

51. Think outside the box.

- Hand out material at top five federal metro stations

- Movie theater preview ads

- Fly a banner over Maryland and Jersey beaches

52. Partner with complementary vendors and share the marketing costs.

53. Radio spots on WTOP.

54. Try metro cards if slots available during busy season.

55. Update any information on GSA Advantage, ProNet, etc.

56. Visit http//:ssq.gsa.gov—run a current report on your GSA Schedule category, regardless of whether you have a Schedule. See who is leading, and look at their web site, ads, etc.

57. Get in MarkeTips. This is the GSA publication that goes to all offices that buy off Schedule.

58. Buy AdWords.

59. Remember, busy season runs into mid-Oct if the budgets are approved—offer a first of the FY special.

60. Don't try and do it all, pick what works for you and execute!

61. Survey says…conduct customer satisfaction measurement after FY close.

62. Schedule an end-of-FY post-mortem: bring in Amtower for a Federal Marketing Audit or the Government Marketing Best Practices workshop.

CHAPTER TEN

Incidental Information:
Some Helpful Things That Really Don't Fit Anywhere Else

Presentation Training:

Some comments on face-to-face and telesales. Absolutely everyone in your organization needs presentation training, from the CEO on down. Anybody that has a face to the public requires presentation training. They have to know how to speak clearly and succinctly. You have to be giving the same message regardless of whom you're talking to. The materials used for this training have to be reviewed and updated regularly. The people who are best at this should be modeled. You have to look at them and see what they do differently, and incorporate this into the training. The training needs to be regular, and really, mandatory for all. If you bust your butt and get your CEO a speaking slot at a key industry event and they are not capable of communicating succinctly to this audience, you're going to destroy, not develop, marketshare.

Telesales:

A quick aside on the tele-web connection. Your telesales staff should be trained, on the inbound especially, and outbound if necessary, if they know that the person they're speaking with is on the web, volunteer to walk them through the web site. Up to and including the purchase process, up to the shopping cart. Do not walk them through the shopping cart, unless they ask for the help. But this will compress the sale cycle and it will incredibly help you in the customer's ability to navigate your web site.

The telesales staff should also be trained to regularly ask that quick three-question survey: what do you read, what do you belong to, what do you attend? This can be a drop-down menu on their computer screen, and when you see it drop down, fill in the blanks. And if they're already filled in, verify them. Ask them to say again, without prompt, the unaided question, what do you read, what do you belong to, what do you attend? Not, do you still read Federal Computer Week? Oh, yeah, of course.

Web Search:

Don't forget about google.com/unclesam. This is an extraordinary tool. And if you use phrases in the search, put the phrase inside quotes to retain the integrity of the phrase. Then go to the bottom of the page on the first page of the results —

especially if there are like 10,000 results – go to the bottom and use the "Search within results." Use a key word, or use another phrase. I've done this to find special interest groups, competitor info, your company info, key players in the market to develop niche lists for customers. It is an extraordinary tool. Viewing carefully the top 10 to 20 sites on this search, on the Google search, can yield really, really good information, but it takes a lot of time to do this. So if you're going to play with the google.com/unclesam function, make sure you block out – no telephone calls, no other interruptions – at least 30 to 45 minutes to do it, and give yourself a very specific task to research. You'll be extremely pleased—and probably amazed—at the results.

The key words, the advertising words for the webs, can be purchased either at google.com or overture.com.

Competitive Intelligence:

Do you know who your major competitors are, and what are you doing to monitor them? Do you know where they exhibit, advertise, network and speak? Do you know what their clients say about them? Are you as good as they are? Do you have a way to gather this information and share it internally?

You have to **monitor the competition**. Marketing and sales staff should be tasked with monitoring key competitors and sharing that information internally. If you have a half a dozen competitors, two-people teams should meet regularly to see what the competitor is doing on the web site, what they're using via direct mail, where they're exhibiting, what articles have been written about them, how many press mentions they've gotten. And you should have an internal means of sharing this information, perhaps on a quarterly basis.

Geographic Considerations/SmartPay:

The federal market is usually divided into eight or 10 federal regions, depending on the agencies. There are 27 cities with more than 20,000 federal employees, and most of these cities have Federal Executive Boards.

There are about **315,000 SmartPay** small purchase cardholders among the feds. And a lot of state and local governments are using the credit cards as well, but not the SmartPay card. NASPO, the National Association of State Purchasing Officials (www.naspo.org) sometimes has information on the state and local government purchase card programs. But purchasing is beginning to centralize, and there are 37,000 occupied civilian sites in the continental U.S. All of the activity does not occur in Washington, D.C.

Other Items:

Address verification for your database should occur with each customer contact. Update all of the data that you have collected at least once every year. Date the information to make certain that nobody is left behind. When you ask for the e-mail address during this update information collection, ask for permission to use the e-mail just for you.

There are a variety of **listings** out there that are free. The *Government Executive* Annual Federal Technology Source is a free listing for IT vendors. Contact www.govexec.com to find out about this. *Government Computer News* has one with paid advertising, but it's distributed to a variety of people inside the government at no cost, so this could be good. It's also available online.

Ethical gray areas. This is information that you can get or verify at usoge.gov, the Office of Government Ethics. Fifty dollar per year limit on gifts on a per employee basis. 20 dollar maximum per gift, including tax. No cash or cash equivalent, ever. Sweepstakes are okay, as long as there are no artificial parameters, if they're open to everyone. And these are sweepstakes that you see normally at trade shows.

Finally, **beware of the corporate ad agency syndrome**. These are largely advertising agencies with little or no real experience in the government market. There are only a couple of agencies in the Washington, D.C. area that truly have extraordinary bandwidth when it comes to understanding the government market, and going with the wrong firm for your major marketing and advertising dollar expenditure can destroy absolutely everything your federal field sales organization has built up. It will not support them; it will destroy them. We've seen it time and again.

Each element of your marketing program has to be **reviewed on a regular basis** — quarterly, at least twice a year. And just as necessary, based largely again on the feedback of your advocates and apostles. And remember the Vic Hunter model: 12 to 18 contacts per year to convert that prospect, and 24 to 36 contacts per year for customer retention.

The idea is to be pervasive, not intrusive, and the goal is to create gravitational pull.

Reinforce your name recognition. Exploit the right venues at trade shows. Look at the one-book buy. Use snail mail. Update your web site. Send trinkets with your shipments — pens and post-its are great; everybody uses post-its. If you want a strong leave-behind, let me very strongly recommend the Federal Personnel Guide. Each of these contacts adds up.

This is not a stagnant market. Work at staying current. Read the publications, attend the briefings, the seminars. Subscribe to my newsletter, the Amtower B-to-G Market Report. Attend this seminar. The seminar version of this book goes around the country every year, and it's updated every year.

Government marketing best practices are not stagnant. And this book will be revised and re-issued in about a year and a half.

For reading all this, I have a guarantee. It is simple: you can call me anytime with any government marketing-related question, and if I do not know the answer, I will find someone that does.

Amtower's Sixth Law: Positioning can be done by you, for you, or to you.

The choice is yours.

Good luck and good hunting!

Appendix 1: Resources

Marketing Resources

Amtower & Company: Government Marketing Specialists and Federal mailing list compiler. http://www.FederalDirect.net

B2Gov.com: business development and sales for the Federal market. http://www.b2gov.com

By Appointment Only: outbound telemarketing firm specializing in high-level appointment making. http://www.baoinc.com

Capital Reps: GSA Schedule Negotiation & Schedule Management services. http://www.CapitalReps.com

Colmar Corporation: provides assistance to government IT contractors in several ways:

- Through its federal forecast Service, the Total Accumulated Forecast of Federal Information Systems, COLMAR provides detailed IT spending estimates, by program and year, for more than 80 federal agencies.

- COLMAR updates this forecast monthly, in response to mandated changes from the

123

Congress, the oversight agencies, or the program agencies themselves.

- COLMAR collects an extensive library of federal IT planning and budgeting documents which are not available online. COLMAR then makes these available to clients.

- COLMAR provides custom market analysis in such areas as vendor market shares, technology penetration (in support of mergers and acquisitions), and detailed agency analysis.

- COLMAR provides this information to small government contractors at unbeatable rates. http://www.colmarcorporation.com

Compliance Core: Compliance Core is a single source for drug and alcohol testing and DNA testing services. We provide our clients with not only the devices but also coordinate lab services, collection facilities and Medical Review Officer Services.

On the state level and more and more on the federal level, contractors are required to have a Drug Free Workplace program in effect to receive the awards. Some states actually give companies a discount on their Workers Comp insurance if they have a drug and alcohol testing program. http://www. compliancecore.com

JoAnna Brandi's Customer Care Coach: What a Difference One Hour Makes! In just one hour a week you can learn how to: Increase your customer loyalty, decrease your employee turnover, get more business from existing customers and get lots of new referrals, all for only a dollar a day.

HOW? By enrolling in JoAnna Brandi's Customer Care Coach! This weekly training and coaching program gives managers all the tools they need to have their teams create more value, better customer experiences & profits! To find out more, visit http://www.customercarecoach.com

Dragonfly Design: web site design and development. http://www.dragonfly-design.com

ENC Marketing: marketing and advertising specialists for government. http://www.encmarketing.com

Eagle Eye: provider of government contract and grant data. http://www.eagleeyeinc.com

EZ Compliance: An automated tool to produce the proposal Compliance Matrix Report. This incredibly powerful piece of software is now available for Section C of RFPs and is designed to save time and money on your proposal preparation. Click here to try it!

Federal Business Council: Government Conference and In-Agency table-top show producer. Federal Business Council, Inc. has been the industry leader in federal government on-site information technology expositions and conferences since 1976. Conducting more than 150 events per year, we give you a comprehensive forum to market your products and services directly to federal agencies, military and Department of Defense locations across the country. Special programs for small businesses or any SBA designated special classifications. http://www.fbcinc.com

125

Federal Marketing Associates: marketing services for companies targeting government. http://www.fma-onthemark.com

Fern Krauss Public Relations: Public relations. 301-424-9140 Strategic marketing communications.

Grant Thornton: World-class accounting and management consulting for middle-market companies. Grant Thornton International is the world's leading accounting, tax and business advisory organization dedicated to mid-size companies. Through its network of 585 offices in 110 countries, including 50 offices in the U.S., partners of the member firms of Grant Thornton provide personal attention and seamless service delivery to public and private clients around the globe. Grant Thornton LLP's web site is www.GrantThornton.com.

Input: Government IT contract tracking and consulting service producer. http://www.input.com

Mac McIntosh: BtoB Sales Lead Experts, www.salesleadexperts.com. Sales lead management training and consulting.

Market Connections: IT research studies for Federal contractors. http://www.marketconnectinc.com

Michael A Brown: BtoB By Phone, www.michaelabrown.net. Telemarketing and telesales training and consulting

NCS Direct: full service data processing and direct mail shop. http://www.ncsdirect.com

OCI: proposal management consulting and training; www. orgcom.com

O'Keeffe and Company: full service marketing communications. www.okco.com

Summit Insight: Summit Insight helps Canadian firms win U.S. government contracts by finding opportunities and strengthening strategies for long-term success. Our industry clients capitalize on their uniquely Canadian advantages (and navigate uniquely Canadian problems) in winning contracts in federal, state, or local government, for goods or services, civilian or military. Our Canadian government clients present the most effective programs and resources they've ever offered for these special U.S. markets. www.summitinsight.com

Associations

American Society for Public Administration
www.aspanet.org

National Association of State Personnel Executives
www.naspe.net

National Institute of Governmental Purchasing
http://www.nigp.org/

National Contract Management Association
http://www.ncmahq.org/

Institute for Supply Management (formerly the National Association of Purchasing Management)
http://www.napm.org/

ACT: American Council for Technology
http://actgov.ppc.com

AEA: American Electronics Association
http://www.aeanet.org

AFCEA: Armed Forces Communications & Electronics Association
http://www.afcea.org

IOPFDA: Independent Office Products and Furniture Dealers Association
http://www.iopfda.org

ITAA: Information Technology Association of America
http://www.itaa.org

PSC: Professional Services Council
http://www.pscouncil.org/

Publications

American City and County
www.AmericanCityanD.C.ounty.com
Federal Computer Week
www.fcw.com

Government Computer News
www.gcn.com

Government Executive
www.govexec.com

Governing
www.governing.com

Government Procurement and Government Product News
www.govpro.com

Government Technology
www.govtech.net

Government Video
www.governmentvideo.com

Government Security
www.govtsecurity.securitysolutions.com

Government Security News
www.GSNmagazine.com

Washington Technology
www.washingtontechnology.com

Appendix 2: SmartPay

Federal SmartPay (formerly IMPAC) Credit Card Statistics

Fiscal Year	# of transactions	# of cardholders	Total FY $
1989	47,595	13,032	$9,088,038
1990	331,957	21,431	67,779,471
1991	730,564	35,234	67,747,687
1992	1,097,500	48,819	307,450,342
1993	1,736,373	84,284	537,501,272
1994	2,765,615	96,090	921,639,498
1995	4,246,329	130,353	1,591,836,136
1996	7,000,000+	185,000	2.97 billion
1997	11,500,000	240,000	4.95 billion
1998	16,400,000	340,000	7.95 billion
1999	20,600,000	500,000	10.2 billion
2000	23,500,000	490,000	12.3 billion
2001	25,000,000	410,000	13.8 billion
2002	26,000,000	390,000	15.2 billion
2003	26,500,000	360,000	16.2 billion
2004	26,500,000	310,000	17.1 billion

The credit card is designed primarily for micropurchases – purchases under $2,500. The program was known as I.M.P.A.C. until 1999, when it was changed to SmartPay. IMPAC was a Rocky Mountain Bankcard trademark; SmartPay is owned by GSA.

Benefits of the credit card program for government are cost avoidance over paper-based procurement, and the speed by which government employees can get products and services to accomplish their work. Benefits for vendors are speed of payment and paperwork (PO processing) avoidance.

The growth of this program is expected to continue at a healthy pace for the next several years, especially if the micropurchase limit is raised to $5,000 or $10,000.

Most states and many local governments are also using small purchase credit cards, though with a smaller per-purchase level.

B2B catalogs selling to the government experience an average order size of 15-20% larger order from Federal buyers over their normal B2B buyers.

Amtower & Company maintains a database of Federal credit card buyers that is available through MeritDirect.

Appendix 3: Mailing Myths

Business-to-Government Mailing Myths Unmasked

For several years, many myths and misconceptions have revolved around direct marketing to government. I'm here to dispel the myths and replace them with empirical data based on unparalleled experience, combing mail rooms, watching Federal employees open their mail, and working with hundreds of mailers over the past 15 years.

The information presented here will help you both make and save money, so please pay close attention.

Myth #1: Government mailrooms limit the number of pieces from a single mailer.

Here I can offer a definitive "yes and no." DoD, particularly military base activities, restrict the number of pieces from a single mailer. The rule (published in the *Federal Register* in September of 1987) states that "mail arriving in quantities of 50 or more from a single identifiable mailer need not be distributed."

Though this is the basic ruling, field research over the past several years indicates that the threshold is 20 pieces of mail, arriving any time during a given week — or longer. We have seen some letters from military base mail managers indicating that they count, from week to week, the mail from specific vendors (talk about way too much time on your hands!).

133

So my advice is between 15 and 20 pieces, no closer than six business days apart. If it's in an envelope, you'll have an even better chance of getting through.

I know of no similar restrictions in civilian agencies.

Myth #2: Government managers and decision makers don't read mail.

Absolutely, positively <u>not</u> true. Our research indicates that senior managers in government receive between 65-75 pieces of mail each day (usually in several deliveries, not all at once). They will spend about fifteen seconds with each piece, during which time they'll make a decision to save, route or toss that piece.

The thing that irritates senior managers most is receiving mail that is not germane to what they do. This has always been one of the top complaints we hear from all managers.

Most people (federal, private sector, and at home) will complain about all the "junk" they get in the mail, but the bottom line is, direct marketing drives a significant portion of the economy, and remains the largest motivator behind the growth of the Federal credit card sales.

Regardless of what people say, nearly everyone reads mail. And enough people respond to make it a very profitable method of communication. In government marketing, direct mail is a critical part of the mix.

If it weren't, several top Schedule vendors would not be licensing data from Amtower & Company. And they are.

Myth #3: You have to mail 1st class to the Federal government.

Once again, this misstatement rears its ugly head with alarming regularity.

First class postage is required in only one ZIP code I have found, the headquarters of the Social Security Administration (ZIP code 21235). And this is for a good reason: the mailroom gets lots of mail from its constituents (older Americans), and the mailroom personnel spend most of their time making certain this mail gets routed properly.

So SSA made a decision not to deliver third class mail at this facility. I don't have a problem with this at all.

The most necessary thing you need when mailing to the government is a good (or great) mailing list, complete with whatever routing code the target agency requires.

There are several other "urban legends" around government marketing and contracting we will seek to dispel over the coming months. But as far as direct mail goes, the first critical decision is quality mailing lists. For that, Amtower & Company remains an excellent choice.

Caveat: the list is only *one* part of the equation.

Appendix 4: Ethics

Off-White #14: In the Government Market, It's the Nuances

Many b-to-b companies have stayed out of the government market thinking it is simply too difficult, arcane, and inbred. In part, this is true. But not to the point where it is insurmountable.

A little education goes a long way. Use gratuities for an example.

Take for instance the ability of a b-to-b company to give a business client a book. Nothing extraordinary, but say a $25 business book which, after the customer or prospect reads it, what you are selling becomes abundantly clear.

I've used this technique for years when dealing with business clients.

But I would never use it with a government client.

Government ethics rules are clearly defined by the U.S. Office of Government Ethics (www.usoge.gov). Generally speaking, gratuities for government employees can never be cash, or cash equivalents. A "gift" to a government employee can never exceed $20 in value, including tax. And gratuities to a single employee may not exceed $50 in a calendar year. Paying for a meal for a government employee is generally not acceptable, unless the meal is part of an event where the employee is a participant.

These represent the "high bar." Any government agency can lower the bar, and several do.

Over the years we have witnessed many glaring errors on the part of alleged government marketing veterans, including:

- A major government publication, which, until recently, sent a survey to its readers each year with a dollar attached. Yes, it's only a buck, but I said NO Cash, ever!!

- A major hardware player which sent the "Reengineering" book (so popular a few years back) to several hundred key senior execs. The cover price was well over threshold.

- A major government web mall, whose radio spots offered "government procurement professionals a free Metro card" for signing up at their site. No cash equivalent, remember.

There are more, but this is already going to piss off a few people, and that's my quota for the day.

The point is, intelligent gift giving is good. A recently launched federal web site sent out a postage paid survey, asking key buyers for input prior to launching their site. They included a nice travel mug—well below threshold for almost any agency. They also got a good return on the survey.

138

Simple stuff, slightly arcane, but simple.

If you have doubts about an offer, call someone who would know. Or contact the Office of Government Ethics.

Appendix 5: SIGs

Off-White Paper 15: Face Time:
SIGs & Associations

(This was published in 1998).

One of the arguments used to get money for trade show participation is the "value of face time with customers and prospects." No one argues that face time is valuable—but at what cost?

One of the most underutilized venues for companies selling to (or wanting to sell to) the Federal government in representation in special interest groups (SIGs) and other associations where Federal employees involved in specific areas spend time.

Active participation in these groups gets you lots of quality time with a carefully defined audience—much more than a trade event will ever give you.

But you have to be willing to spend your time. In the 20 or so years I've been involved in the government market, I have found SIGs for just about every niche imaginable: mail managers, IT-ers of *any* stripe, facility managers, transportation managers, publication managers, virtually any audience you are looking for will have a SIG.

Hell, when the Pentagon Mac Users Group re-launched, it got mentioned in the *Wall Street Journal!*

141

One of my favorite groups, where I've spent time making friends for about 10 years is the Special Interest Group on CD/DVD Applications & Technology (SIGCAT, http://www.sigcat.org/).

"Founded in 1986, SIGCAT is the world's largest users group dedicated to educating the public and promoting the growth of applications based on CD and DVD technologies. With over 11,000 members throughout 75 countries, SIGCAT is the largest member of the Federation of Government Information Processing Councils (FGIPC). SIGCAT helps government agencies, corporations, and individuals better understand CD and DVD-based technologies to enhance their information management and data dissemination activities. SIGCAT has evolved from a small user group started at the U.S. Geological Survey to a self-sustaining 501(c)(3) non-profit foundation." The chairman, Jerry McFaul, is one of the nicest and most accessible people I've ever met.

A corporate sponsorship for SIGCAT is $375.00 a year: think you can afford this?

Another group I've spent time with (on and off) for several years is the Industry Advisory Council (IAC, http://www.iaconline.org/). The IAC is the industry advisory group for the Federation of Government Information Processing Councils (FGIPC, http://www.fgipc.org)—of which SIGCAT is a member council.

The IAC represents the 200+ companies which account for 75%+ of the total IT contract dollars awarded by the federal government. When I was advising companies on marketing major contracts, I spent a fair amount of time there. If you want to play in the major government IT contract arena, is this time well spent?

Trade shows generally run from the high five figures to the low seven figures for participation. You could hire someone to participate in the SIGs for the minimal trade show fee, and, if they were any good, you'd be meeting more of the right people in a better setting.

The "problem" with SIGs is they aren't sexy because they are generally "off the radar" and they involve grunt work and extra (non-9-to-5) time.

But the payoffs are real. The government employees you want to meet are there. They see that you care enough to spend real time with them. They become comfortable with you, and, consequently, when they can, they will remember you come purchase time.

The bottom line for SIGs is that there is probably one for the audience you are looking for. And if you want to build relationships with government buyers, there is no better venue.

Appendix 6:
Publication Mania, Parts 1, 2 & 3

Part 1

Off-White Paper 17:
News for the News Impaired

(This was first published in early 2002, right after the announcement of a new government trade publication.)

In 1998, I wrote a second *Off-White* paper on trade shows (Off-White 3.1) about the soon to be ill-fated GovTechNet. The overall point of that piece was "where is the value-add" for this event—what's the point? We already have two big events, and unless you're targeting a strong niche, there is no need for this. Well, I pissed off a few people. Again.

And, the event folded in short order.

And now we have a similar situation. *The Washington Post* announced 9/23/02 what many of us already knew, that there was another publication being launched in the Federal market. The *Federal Paper* is to be a weekly targeting "senior executives, presidential appointees, and the Hill" (read: the already overworked, the learning impaired, & the otherwise unemployable) with news that apparently they aren't getting elsewhere. A controlled circulation base of 30,000 of people who need yet another news source.

145

The breakdown: 7,000+ presidential appointees (deer-in-the-headlights syndrome); the Hill, 1,000-2,000 (with news about the executive branch? They already know everything they want to know, which they get from *The Idiot's Guide to the Executive Branch*); 5,000+ career SES people (my God, people who work!) and another 15,000 "senior" people (AARP?)

News in Washington, D.C. which they aren't getting elsewhere? Well, of course, there is no news for these people in *Roll Call, Congressional Quarterly, National Journal, Government Executive, the Post's Federal Page, FCW* or *GCN* and a host of others, including paid newsletters, e-newsletters, web sites and gossip.

That being said, an experienced team has been assembled to pull this off, and it is led by someone with a publishing background.

But the premise remains weak, and when my clients and friends call (I get at least one a day on this one), my advice is "save your money, or if you have that much to spare, give it to me."

So here's how they got there…

Market research: three sycophants and a rich person in a room with a case of Heineken and four straws.

Rich guy: "I think we can make a play in the public sector publishing market."

Sycophant 1: " Oohhh, it's a great market."
Sycophant 2: "Aahhh, it's a huge market."
Sycophant 3: "Yes, but aren't there…"

Rich guy: "You're fired."

Sycophant 1: "Decisive."

Sycophant 2: "Forceful."

Rich guy: "Adjourned."

Come to think of it, I am out of cat litter.

Not that I have an opinion on this....

Part 2

Off-White Paper #20: Publication Mania

(This was first published in early 2003, when CMP announced it was going to launch a trade publication for government. I am not aware the publication ever came out.)

Last fall in Off-White Paper #17, I blasted the *Federal Paper* for entering a market that didn't require what they were offering. They are apparently ceasing publication after less than 6 months. Not a big surprise, but the market is informationally well fed. I didn't think they had a significant enough readership (target was 30,000 "senior" government readers), and my argument was simple: these people are not looking for more to read, and the proposed information was available elsewhere. Insufficient market research.

147

And now, yet another big publisher—CMP—wants to come into the government market.

I receive all three Federal publications but I recently read CMP is starting a government systems book, *Government Enterprise*. It's going to be poly-bagged with *InformationWeek, Network Computing* and *Optimize* and have an initial circulation of 47,000, and it will be a quarterly (I got this from *BtoB*, which is an excellent marketing publication—check out www.btobonline. com). Frequency: quarterly.

My advice to advertisers? Quarterly?

This is the same CMP that, inside *VAR Business*, an otherwise excellent read, started a government reseller magazine last year, not a bad move. You may recall a few years back that *Government Technology* published *Government Reseller* for a couple years (I was a columnist). But one cover of the new *VAR Business* government magazine that caught my attention called CDW-G a "systems integrator." Now I'll be first in line to call CDW-G a savvy player in the government market, but I'd have to stop way short of calling them an integrator. Is this the level of knowledge and expertise we can expect from yet another publication targeting the fewer ad dollars in our otherwise healthy niche? My advice to advertisers: tell them you're a systems integrator and get a cover shot.

So let me poke a little more into the *BtoB* piece on CMP. They are planning a 50/50 split between ad space and editorial, So does this mean we're talking 12 page newsletter or real magazine?

Oh, but Mark, it has a web site too! Who the heck doesn't?

Do I think this is a bad idea? Not necessarily, as there are pockets of government techies reading all types of technical publications. They read these because they are necessarily technically deeper than *Federal Computer Week,* or *Government Computer News,* which are primarily news publications.

There are pockets of government readers in virtually any B2B publication.

But if CMP thinks the government techies will <u>add</u> more to their reading <u>and</u> maintain subscriptions in the *Information Week, Network Computing* and *Optimize* to read the new book, I think they are wrong. We are all limited on our time, and we tend to reduce or condense what we read rather than expand the volume. If CMP doesn't mind losing the subscribers it has to the other books to their new one, they might last a year.

The audit statements of the supplier magazines will suffer in at least two ways if they proceed. First, government buyers almost always spend more than their business counterparts, so the buying influence in dollars in subsequently audit statements would drop if my premise is correct about the Federal readers opting for fewer publications.

Second, the overall numbers of each of the supplier publications would also drop (again, if my premise holds). They say their initial distribution will be 47,000, which averages out to just under 16,000 per publication from the three publications they will draw from.

A better plan might be to add more real government news to three already healthy publications. That would be a value add across the board without depleting the resources of the publisher and taking subscribers away from three relatively healthy publications.

Will *Government Enterprise* last? Probably not. It might outlast the *Federal Paper*, but that won't win bragging rights.

Part 3

Off – White #22:
Yet More Publication Mania, or, Is There a Bandwagon We Haven't Hitched to Yet?

(This was first published later in 2003 after several companies announced new publications, each staking ground to the seemingly lucrative "homeland defense" territory).

Now that Martha Stewart has been let off the SEC hook, she's announced a new publication: *Martha Stewart's Home, Land and Garden Defense Journal.* The cover story is on how to make the clear plastic covering (with duct tape) more attractive on your outer windows using those crinkle-cut scissors, multi-colored duct tape, and some other things lying around the house. A related story is on home-based remedies for bio-terror.

While this may appear to be an exaggeration, I will not be surprised if it really happens.

Pennwell launched *Homeland Security Solutions* in April. The publishers of *The Hill* are coming out with *Government Security News*, and as I recall, there were a couple other security publications last year at the first GovSec as well, including *Loss Prevention & Security Journal*, *Security Magazine*, and *Government Security*. Not dissimilar from a Beijing neighborhood —maybe a little too crowded.

We also have CMP taking subscribers from three healthy publications (Information Week, Network Computing and Optimize) to create the quarterly *Government Enterprise.* eRepublic (the *Government Technology* folks) are starting a public sector CIO publication. The *Federal Paper,* launched in September 2002, didn't last through the end of last year.

There are others, but my brain hurts.

These are attempting to join the usual suspects - the established publications: *Federal Computer Week, Government Computer News,* and *Government Executive* magazine, as well as the e-newsletters of each, including the weekly e-news on Homeland Defense from *Government Executive.*

OK, so the publishing vultures are circling the government market. The rest of the economy has been dead for so long that there's nothing left on the bones. Now these vultures are coming after a live, robust, though slow-moving behemoth. These vultures have *finally* realized that there may be something to this "executive branch" thing.

What does this mean for publishers of established publications, to advertisers, to potential readers, and anyone silly enough to invest?

Publishers: for established publishers, pray that Dell does not lend legitimacy to these pretenders by advertising in any of them. I don't think the Round Rockers will fall for this latest rash of editorial drivel. This (Dell advertising) wouldn't save any of these would-be publications, but it could prolong some of them. Like the *Federal Paper* last year, before busy season 2004 the majority of these newbies will be gone. Some won't survive the slow Federal winter of 2003/04. There simply isn't room, much less the new editorial fodder necessary to create some excitement.

Advertisers: You've all been here before. Some poorly informed sales rep will attempt to speak "government" to you, invariably mess up the acronyms, represent the "tens of thousands" of yet-to-subscribe "security decision makers" their publication will reach (at some nebulous future date), and offer you a deal (and maybe a cover story! With reprints!). Hint: there is a difference between "reader" and "subscriber." Let's wait for an audit from BPA before we express any real thrill about these sales reps interrupting your day.

Potential readers: how many information sources do they want, or need? Who are these as yet unreached, under-informed readers? I don't think many in the public sector will bother to subscribe to these, as they already get lots of information from many sources and most don't wish to add to their reading lists. Well, the Hill might subscribe. They always like free publications where they might get mentioned, or quoted. And they can get a reprint! If one book stands out editorially, they might have a chance. Maybe.

Investors: anyone putting outside money into one of these is foolish, plain and simple. Don't get me wrong, I miss foolish investors. I sold their dot-coms lots of data a few years back. Any major publishing firm entering this arena thinking they can establish marketshare better take a close look at the three Federal publications and ask themselves why any intelligent advertiser would migrate to untested waters when most of them are spending less anyway.

Haven't had enough? Well then, let's look at the rather adjectival Media Kit for *Government Security News*.

The target audience is "39,000 security-related integrators, resellers, government security buyers at GS-12 and above" (GS-12 is government-speak!) at the "federal level but also major state, county and municipal governments across the U.S." It promises to reach more "government security executives" (new OPM functional designation?) "than any other publication." I can tell from the "bona fides" of the staff that these are carefully selected readers. *The Hill* will scour its records for all those GS-12s who have testified on the Hill. 39,000 *is* a magic number, though. Everyone on *The Hill* knows this.

The letter from the publisher, Edward Tyler (yes, *the* Edward Tyler! I never heard of him, either.) offers a *personal* commitment to helping you "garner your fair share of the growing government market for your security products, systems and related services." Husker-du! If that isn't comforting, I don't know what is!

And that's not all—they have an "exclusive e-mail research program," for which you have to contact your account rep to get details. Sounds like research on how much money you might have that they can get...

Apparently you can order your reprints now! "Call our Reprint Manager to order reprints!" They have a *manager* for reprints—great! Maybe that's another new OPM job function area. I know several Congressmen who have already called for reprints, while others are asking for Reprint Managers for their staffs.

Then there's the free e-mail program—they'll e-mail "5,000 of our subscribers (a $1500 value)." Would you like spam with your toast?

The editorial calendar promises many things (access control, ID technology, intrusion detection, data information security) that evidently aren't available elsewhere. And may not be available here if you believe they'll be around in the six months they're projecting this calendar.

Market research for the launch of this publication? My guess is that editors of *The Hill* started getting curious about that "executive branch thing" that kept interrupting our illustrious Congresspeople from their respective headline chasing.

"What do you suppose they're talking about?"

"I don't know. Whatever it is, it isn't on the *Hill*."

"Do you suppose it's one of those other branches they talk about?"

"Well if it is, it can't be as much fun as watching these ambulance chasers up here."

"Send Tyler."

Anyone see Peter Weller and John Lithgow in *The Adventures of Buckaroo Banzai*?

"Where are we going?"

"Planet 10!"

"When are we going?"

"Real soon!"

Now let's talk Defense. I know companies that want some defense against the idiots crawling out of the woodwork trying to launch a bunch of Home, Land and Garden Defense and Security publications.

Appendix 7:
Trade shows: Parts 1, 2, & 3

Part 1:

Off-White Paper #3 Events - To Show or Not to Show

(First published in 1998, this was my first major piece asking if big trade shows were justified marketing expenses.)

Face-to-face works for selling. No one can argue with this.

But, when faced (no pun intended) with ever-dwindling marketing budgets (who are the morons who don't invest in marketing, anyway?), and the ever-rising costs of participating in trade shows, MarComs (marketing communication managers) have hard choices to make.

Trade shows cost money for the space, the booth, the pre/at/ post show marketing, hotels, people (man hours away from other activities), training booth personnel (if you're going to do this right), and much more.

And trade shows offer: what percentage of your target market? What guarantee that you'll have the right people find your booth in the midst of 400-500 other booths (of thousands of booths, if you are considering exhibiting at Comdex).

Let's take FOSE. Here is an event which emerged from a long

war with several other (now mostly defunct) events (FCC, Federal ADP, GCN Expo, etc) to dominate the government/ Washington spring timeframe. The published attendance numbers when FOSE was owned by National Trade Productions (NTP) were over 70,000. It doesn't matter whether or not you believe these numbers, because those of us who were there experienced crowded aisles, long registration lines (for those silly enough not to pre-register), and relatively happy exhibitors. Before NTP sold the event, they attempted to re-focus (or de-focus, depending on your point of view) the event into "America's Computer Show", not a government event.

Mistake #1. Cahners/Reed exacerbated the problem by marketing FOSE like their other major event, the Auto Show. Well, boys and girls: D.C. ain't Detroit and Computers aren't cars (though they are commodities), and the attendance started to drop.

To PNBI's (Post Newsweek Business Information, the new owner) credit, the event is focused exclusively on government once again. But the rising cost of the space coupled with the lower attendance make it a difficult option for many vendors. For most, money is better spent at smaller, more focused events, like the table-top events produced by the Federal Business Council and IT Direct. For others, spending more money on space and direct mail makes more sense.

With government purchasing becoming more decentralized, spending a large portion of your budget on one event in one location (even Washington), is no longer a viable option.

And look at the new flies in the ointment. Federal Computer Week is launching a spring event in 1999, GovTech, three weeks after FOSE (see "Off-White" 3.1), targeting virtually the same vendors and going after the same attendees. And there are rumors about them adopting the marketing of the shrinking AFCEA events, especially TechNet.

And last summer, eGov, produced by IT Direct and the omnipresent Israel Feldman, attracted 10,000 government employees in the now vacant summer slot (which used to be owned by NTP with FedMicro, a story for another time).

CEOs generally don't understand marketing (which is why it almost always ends up subordinate to sales). But they (CEOs) seem to be under the spell of the "gotta be at this event in a big way" bug when they see certain competitors at allegedly significant events. These "marketing epiphanies" often occur after a meal with the trade show producers, and are the bane of Marcoms everywhere.

In my estimation, events need to be focused to be of value. But if they are too focused, say on a particular technology, they becomes "sunset" events. When the technology is no longer cutting edge, the lights go out on the show.

SIGCAT, the Special Interest Group for CD Rom Applications & Technologies, hosts an annual event that attracts 2,000+ key people in CD Rom based technologies, especially government people. This has been going on since the mid 1980s, and there has been a steady migration to and expansion of the technology. But it is focused. FedUnix (anyone remember this show?) was focused on the government use of Unix, and the exhibitors and attendees alike were pleased with the event precisely because of the focus. But the technology went South, and the show died.

Comdex (which has had defections) and FOSE (which has had some defections), may or may not be passe. But I believe that for FOSE (or any event) to continue and grow, it needs to focus on more than just "government" ("Uh, we're here to facilitate the implementation of beneficial technologies designed to bring service to the citizens"...See "Off-White" paper on WPI). There has to be some true value add for both the exhibitor and the attendee if shows of this size can truly justify themselves to the MarComs who have so little money and so much to do.

And with eGov and GovTech entering the fray, vendors (and their respective MarComs) will have more difficult decisions to make.

Let's make a checklist for the important things to look for when selecting an event, and I'll post your comments.

Part 2:

FOSE, the "Big Bag Theory," The Creation of Myths and Marketing Myopia: Off-White Paper #21

(This was first published in May, 2003, immediately following the FOSE event.)

Many things occurred at FOSE this year.

For those who don't know, FOSE is the grand-daddy of and sole survivor of the government computer conference wars (George Lucas stole the idea and put it in outer space).

In the beginning (in a galaxy far, far away), there was the Federal ADP Show (which evolved into FOSE), FedUnix, Federal Computer Conference, GCN Expo, FedMicro, GovProExpo, GovTechNet, and eGov (which also survives, but isn't really a computer show). Lots of shows, for when computers were young and sexy, not mundane and pervasive.

FOSE was held at the new Washington Convention Center. Darn good thing for those signs and staff to direct us. The Convention Center is huge, and while FOSE is adequately sized by D.C. trade show standards (though it is barely one third of its early 1990s size), it is small in the Convention Center. They were able to fill a significant hall, though, but it was not so crowded as to seem rushed either day I was there.

FOSE's radio spot touted the "tens of thousands" of attendees expected. Tens of tens, definitely. Tens of hundreds, yes. Tens of thousands—no way. If they were including all of the workers and Convention Center staff, and the cabbies and pedestrians in the immediate vicinity, they might break (barely) into the multiple "tens" category—with two tens. Maybe.

FOSE's main direct mail promotional effort was an oversized post card with a picture of kids trick-or-treating. The caption: "What you won't find at FOSE."

Call it literary license, hyperbole, or wishful thinking: their advertising could fertilize small countries.

What did we see at FOSE was hundreds of people lined up for worthless toys, trinkets, bags, and other alleged goodies. And yes, I got my fair share, though not from the "house." MicroWarehouse knew the "trick or treaters" would be there and catered to them. The "house" had the most booth traffic, a perpetual line waiting to get into the inner sanctum of trinket-dom "Oh Look! A flashlight! On a key ring! How unique!" "And not one T-shirt, but two. A very manly pink and baby barf green." Here in the inner sanctum, they also asked people to trade their CDW bags for MicroWarehouse bags, a stunt pulled by CDW on GTSI when the new MicroWarehouse crew was at CDW. Juvenile, yes, but "oh so annoying."

Do decision-makers have time to stand in line for trinkets? None that I know, and I have never seen any senior people waiting in line at any show since the early 1990s, and very few then.

This is branding?

Word on the floor was the "House" spent around $1,000,000, all told. When FOSE saw them coming, the voice at the drive-thru asked: "Would you like to super-size that?"

But the Bag Wars…

The Big Bag Theory

The theory goes something like this: He with the most, the biggest, brightest bag wins. Wins "what," we're not sure. Maybe wins bragging rights to whose bag will annoy more people on the subway, make it harder to get into and out of cabs, fill up more trash cans (and there were hundreds in trash containers in the Convention Center), hold more cat litter, or win the annual

Amtower Award for Big Bag?

The "battle of the bags" also did not disappoint. The official results:

CDW-G, biggest overall bag at 18x24x8 (qualifies as a luxury hotel room in the far East); MicroWarehouse, second with 19x21x8.25; GSTI, third with 15x22x6.

Brightest bag: I still think CDW-G has the brightest with the bright yellow and red. My wife said the Warehouse pink and yellow bag is as bright. So it's a toss-up.

But here is what I saw on the floor: many MicroWarehouse bags all over the floor, and about 25% of them inside the CDW-G bags; some GTSI bags on the floor (tropical pastels, they were harder to spot), and a few others much less conspicuous.

My favorite bag? The Exabyte bag, as it was the only canvas bag (13x16x4.5) available at the show, and I had several people ask me where I got it.

And in the trash cans on the way out of the convention center? Hundreds of big bags.

The annual Amtower Award for Big Bag winner, and the winner of the battle of the bags, is GovConnection. I saw their marketing manager on the first day of the show, and he told me they weren't exhibiting, but saving their money for more tactical efforts.

MicroWarehouse also had a mini-blimp floating around the hall (apparently radio controlled).

Which leads to...

The Creation of a Myth

On the last day of the show, Alan Bechara (GM of PC Mall's government division) was at the Exabyte booth. Here, he was dive-bombed by the MicroWarehouse blimp. The usually quiet and unassuming Bechara pivoted, and planted a right cross smack on the nose of the blimp, whereupon it promptly deflated.

Ain't nobody gonna mess with "One-Punch Al" anymore. Stand back, here comes the man who took out MicroWarehouse with a single punch. I have a new hero, the Jedi, "One Punch" Bechara.

I understand several MicroWhiners followed him to his booth (well out of right cross range), complaining of mistreatment. They even brought a FOSE security guard over, who questioned him at a distance, also staying out of range.

When "One Punch" feinted toward them, they all ran screaming into "tens of tens" crowding the aisles. "One Punch" Bechara, able to leap small booths in a single bound...

Which leads to...

Marketing Myopia

Big shows eat big bucks. Period. Attendance is down at major events across the board. Comdex filed for bankruptcy.

Big computer shows are dinosaurs. They serve no useful purpose, except to fill the coffers of those saying "if you're not here, you're not a player."

FOSE has no focus. If it did, it would have a tag line, one that made sense and was much better than "Technology Unites Us." The only thing that got united at FOSE was the "I hate

164

MicroWarehouse" club. What the "house" probably doesn't understand is that in irritating lots of people, they (MicroW) united them (other resellers) against a common foe. Kind of like Napoleon: too many fronts.

One CEO was heard complaining to his staff about being dwarfed and "out-marketed" by the "House," and not letting this happen next year: what can they do to be bigger at FOSE next year?

Wrong question. A better question is why care about a D.C.-centric show full of trinket collectors? Why not spend your money on tactical marketing, smaller events that are less cluttered and where real face time with real customers occurs?

Another PC vendor complained about the lack of uniformed personnel. I know that the Federal Business Council hosted an event at the Defense Intelligence Agency Thursday (the last day of FOSE) and had over 300 people. And the same day at Hanscom AFB, they had 275. You want uniformed personnel—go where they are, especially when many of them are deployed.

Dell, the largest of the IT vendors, had a modest presence, actually behind Micron PC (now MPC). Taking a cue from Compaq, which pulled out several years ago. I'm wagering Dell won't be at FOSE next year. Think it'll hurt their #1 Schedule 70 standing? Not a chance.

It is not a crime not to exhibit at FOSE. The argument that "you're not a player unless you're there" wasn't valid when there were 50,000 attendees, and is less so now.

The real question is how much of your money can you throw

away being ignored in a large exhibit hall, versus the number of tactical events you could do for the same money. Or the amount of direct mail you could send. Or how you can finally get around to creating a great web site, as opposed to having it on your "to do" list.

MicroWarehouse was as close to show domination as you can get, except...that in the Exhibitor Guide, even though they had a full page advertisement, their listing in the alpha-portion of the Guide was plain vanilla—no colored box like many other exhibitors.

And the Exhibitor Guide has more shelf life than the big bags.

Part 3:

FOSE, The Event Phenomena, and the Divine Right to Attention, Off-White #24

(This was published in the fall of 2004 to serve as a review of the many events in 2004, and their respective values.)

* Surgeon general's warning: Reading this Off-White paper can cause upset stomachs and lead to ulcers—if you produce events. It will lead to other stomach problems if you are an industry observer and an exhibitor at industry events. These problems will relate to spasms and cramps caused by laughter and choking.

There are hundreds of events weekly in Washington, D.C., and I assume the same is true around the country, though perhaps to a lesser degree when it comes to government-focused events. It would be possible to spend one's professional life going from event to event, never setting foot in an office.

This has been the state of affairs here in the 20-plus years I have been in the market, and it is not likely to change. Events are good things, especially when produced by people wired into our insular market, and when the event offers significant return on time investment (ROTI) for all involved. Cost becomes less relevant if the ROTI factor is strong.

As we know, not all events are created equal, nor are all event producers wired into this community. It could even be postulated that some event producers are here simply for the money. Throughout this paper I will name names. I cannot name all events that are good, nor will I name all events that are, in my opinion, borderline or outright bad. I will simply highlight a few that stand out in my mind, or stick in my craw.

These are my opinions, nothing more, nothing less. These opinions have been honed over 20 years in this market. I have been (and remain) an event producer, an attendee of hundreds of events, a member of Boards of Advisors (FOSE and eGov, at different times), and an advisor to companies that spend serious money selecting events to support. Although I write to amuse both myself and you, I also write to educate—again both you and me—on the nuances that make some venues better than others, and render other events useless. I focus and learn more every time I write. I trust you will learn and perhaps share your lessons with me and others.

That being said, *here I go again…*

The Divine Right to Attention

Each week, many people forward me e-mails touting events:
new events, established events, "agency sponsored" events, CIO
level events, special interest group events, and events with so
many adjectives in the description that you feel the producer
is exerting a *divine right to your attention*. They evidently feel
they have this divine right as they spam you with hyperbole
attempting to position themselves as the sole savior and
provider of your business opportunities. If you read the e-copy,
you might believe (and some actually do) that this (never before
produced) event will deliver the absolute right people at a time
designated by no less an authority than Nostradamus *and* will
produce results that will make Bill Gates, Michael Dell and Sam
Walton envious. Sign up at www.GiveMeYourGovMoney.com.

When you receive many of these announcements, and if you
accept the carefully crafted adjectival assertions, you would
immediately know that if you are not at this particular event
that life would not simply pass you by, but that your career
would come to a screeching halt. Time for the cyanide.

Sometimes these invitation/announcements amuse me, and
other times I become incensed at the apparent arrogance of
the purveyors of this crap. I spend a great deal of time writing
about events for the simple reason that *relationships are absolutely
key* in the B2G arena, and the proper event venue can help create
and maintain relationships. I also write about this because there
are so many events that are, at best, suspect in their respective
claims. These are the *blue sky* events.

Oh – geez, here goes Amtower off on a tangent *already*....
relationships? What is this, Dr Phil?

Not at all. The connection between relationships and events
is palpable. There is no better venue than the *right* event with
the *right people* for relationship building. And there is nothing
more important in this market than building and maintaining
the right relationships to grow your business. Events, special
interest groups and associations are three of the main ways we
meet key people and develop relationships.

In a largely overlooked book, *The Anatomy of Buzz*, Emanuel
Rosen dissects the real power of word-of-mouth marketing
and the true reach of the impact of 'buzz," then spends the
rest of the book showing how to *create* and *manage* word-
of-mouth (buzz) marketing. This is one of the few truly
indispensable marketing books (http://www.federaldirect.net/
recommendedreading.html), as it offers the best advice available
on cost-free advertising.

So where does this bring us?

Events cost money. Period. Big events usually cost big money.
This does not mean they are not useful, but the *proper use* of
events by those attending, exhibiting, or speaking, rarely occurs.
Exploiting an event to create "buzz" around you, your booth,
your product/service or company is critical. Managing this
buzz at and after the event is a manageable process I will deal
with separately. Or you can read the book.

For those who read my now infamous Off-White 21, "FOSE,
The Big Bag Theory, and the Creation of Myths" (http://www.
federaldirect.net/offwhite21.html), you know that I thought

FOSE 2003 was overrun by MicroWarehouse. This was only partially correct on my part. MicroWarehouse was attempting to create "buzz," and they were successful. What they were not successful at was the _management_ of that buzz. It backfired big-time because they irritated so many people. When Off White 21 came out, there was a groundswell of support for my position because it validated what so many already thought, especially the other exhibitors at FOSE 2003. Off-White 21 became the most visited page on my web site for months, and remains popular today, a year and a half later.

There are many legitimate venues out there, events with a history, a track record that you can see. There are event producers with a pedigree, who at the request of real government agencies, will produce actual events. FOSE is among the events with history. I was on the Board of Advisors in the early 1990s (1992-94). While I think FOSE has peeked, there are those who feel strongly that "the show must go on," and this is not simply the show producers.

Spontaneous Generation

Many of the _blue sky_ event producers may actually have some track record elsewhere, in another industry. Somewhere, perhaps over the rainbow, under a beautiful blue sky that rains money. They assume, by the alleged success in other markets, that when they announce _their_ event in _our_ market, the people will line up. We have all been waiting for your parade to come to town before we do anything. The _blue sky_ events assume the announcement alone will spontaneously generate attendance akin perhaps to spinning gold from straw. D.C. is after all, the spin capitol of the universe. Or the _blue sky events_ assume _you will think_ their name will instantly generate attendance, so you will send them a check immediately to be a part of this historic event. If you spend enough, your company logo might even appear on the plaque bestowed by National Historic Trust.

Many of these events are produced by P.T. B;
Marcus Evans, for instance, seems to think tl
sale, or at least for rent. Attend the Evans ev
and you can meet privately with several CIOs. Evans
the CIOs mistaken for Capitol Hill denizens, many of whom are
for rent, especially in an election year.

Individual Events and Producers

There are several legitimate, pedigreed government event
producers in this market. The publications (*Federal Computer
Week, Government Computer News*, and *Government Executive*)
produce events. The Federal Business Council and the
Digital Government Institute produce events. These are
all organizations that are hard-wired into government and
industry and produce potentially valuable events. If you look
at the Board of Advisors for the Digital Government Institute
(www.digitalgovernment.com), you will see 23 of the heaviest
hitters from government and industry. I was invited to one
meeting to discuss marketing and the input from these people
for Ms. Nelson's program is truly extraordinary. The Federal
Business Council (FBC, www.fbcinc.com) offers the broadest
penetration of government from an in-agency (on site) basis of
any event producer, and the venues are not simply the half-day
tabletops for which FBC is known. At the request of several
cabinet departments, FBC does high-level, multi-day agency
specific events.

There are a variety of smaller events, like the breakfast and
after-work cocktail seminars produced by many industry
contributors, like CMA and ENC Marketing. Immix produces
excellent sales seminars, OCI produces great proposal seminars.
Input and Federal Sources host regular briefings from specific
CIOs and others. Amtower & Company (that would be me)
produces perhaps the best B2G marketing seminar (soon to

ook). The list goes on and on. There are simply *too many* ention, even if they are worthwhile, and you cannot and iould not attend all of them.

The people driving some of these are impressive: Lorenz Hassenstein of PostNewsWeekTech and FOSE has very impressive trade show credentials. Mike Smoyer of Federal Computer Week and the eGov Institute has equally impressive credentials. I actually met Mike way back when he worked for the original FOSE owner. Christina Nelson of the Digital Government Institute was the conference director for FOSE when Mike Smoyer was there, and Eva Neumann of ENC Marketing was the marketing director of FOSE. I was fortunate enough to be on the FOSE Board of Advisors at that time. Equally impressive but sometimes less visible are the two powers at FBC: Mike O'Neil and David Powell. Mike works the government side, while David works the industry side, and FBC has been around a long time. These are all people I like and respect, and who have a proven track record of adding value to our community.

Enough sucking up, Amtower, on to the dirt!

FOSE

Consider this the belated FOSE analysis. FOSE 2004 has come and gone. I believe this is year 28.

Let me start this by saying up front that I am not a fan of huge trade shows for most of my clients. There are several reasons, but it boils down to this: most companies do not adequately prepare for the event, plan ahead or execute properly at trade shows. Everyone should read Barry Siskind's books on trade show selection and marketing. Large trade shows cost big money, and simple things like booth staff training often does not occur. At FOSE, there are a variety of opportunities (special interest group meetings, technical briefings, various pavilions and demonstration areas) that you can participate in to get exposure to audience segments. Simple pre-show marketing to drive targeted traffic to your booth, or to separate meetings with your key staff, either does not occur or occurs in a haphazard fashion.

FOSE remains the single largest event for the Federal information technology community, and if you manage your participation properly, it can bring significant results. If you do little or no active marketing management pre-show, at show or post-show, you are wasting significant funds. This does not mean that those funds could not be better spent elsewhere, depending on what and how you sell to the government.

That being said, here are my FOSE 2004 impressions.

I was not there for opening day, but reports from trusted friends said traffic was good. I was there for day two, and traffic was pretty good.

The "battle of the bags" was a blow-out. CDW-G dominated the show floor with the large yellow and red bag. The only competitor close was GSTI's white bag with a large red circle, displaying the new tag line "I rely on GTSI." I would guess CDW-G had a 10-to-1 advantage on the show floor for the bags, and a huge color advantage. CDW-G bags stood out; the GTSI bags did not, even with the big red circle. It was pointed out to me that the GTSI bag resembled the Japanese flag, a subliminal message GTSI might want to avoid.

In the battle for show floor domination, PC Mall added a twist, having the PC Mall logo on every aisle number sign. They also spent some money to have a banner that was a little wider than the CDW-G and GTSI banners, where all three were hung at the bottom of the escalator where most people came down to the show floor. Did anyone notice the extra size? It had to be pointed out to me. The larger question here is this: does visual domination of an event translate into marketshare? Alan Bechara (a friend of mine who heads up the Mall-Gov effort) needs to read Rosen's book before the next show. If significant "buzz" can be created around the visual dominance, then it can be prolonged and managed after the event.

For better or worse, there was a void due to the absence of MicroWarehouse. The now-defunct MicroWarehouse (whose bag literally and figuratively fit inside the CDW-G bag in 2003) spent $1.2 million on all aspects of FOSE in 2003, from various at-show promotions to hotel room keys with the Warehouse logo, big bags in two colors and two t-shirts. Visually and in many other ways, MicroWarehouse dominated FOSE in 2003. While amusing in some respects, it was a waste, because while they created massive on-site "buzz," no one managed or directed it during or after the event. Further, most of the buzz was negative, the result of the sophomoric pranks (see Off-White #21).

I got a personal tour of FOSE 2004 from David Greene (president of PostNewsWeekTech) and Lorenz Hassenstein. I have spent some time with Mr. Hassenstein since FOSE discussing the event industry in general and FOSE in particular. He has some good ideas for revitalizing FOSE. While I still consider this event something of a dinosaur, Mr. Hassenstein may have the skills to build an ecosystem to support the beast.

GovSec

GovSec, now in its third year, still lacks many of the accoutrements of a major event. It does not have an official show guide or an official publication sponsor, though one publication exhibiting certainly indicated differently. The event is produced by National Trade Productions (NTP), the company that started FOSE in the late 1970s. Bob Harar is still CEO of NTP, and industry veteran Denise Medved heads GovSec. I enjoy the event for a variety of reasons, not the least of which it is focused on security issues, both cyber and physical. Attendance, while not massive, is good. It is not how many people you get, but the quality of each attendee.

GovVideo

This is an event put on by an established publication (Government Video), but a weak event nonetheless. I like walking the exhibit hall (when I attend), but only because I enjoy all of the new video technology. I did not attend this year (I was out of town speaking at yet another event), but reports from reliable sources tell me traffic was weak.

itsGov

Here I am perplexed. While technically I was on a Board of Advisors and a Track Chair, I was not consulted the way I previously have been. The event was held at the Reagan Center, but I remain unsure if it was focused on the government buyer for end of FY (it was an August event), or if it was an educational event (four tracks, each offering valuable information), or both.

Mike Smoyer of the eGov Institute was probably experimenting, which is good, but the execution was not on target. Perhaps this was because of the date being too late in the FY to attract many from either the government or industry side.

175

Associations and SIGs

I would be criminally remiss if I did not mention several of the key groups in our market. AFCEA has events world-wide, and the monthly luncheons for the Bethesda (Maryland) chapter are reportedly great networking opportunities.

AFFIRM, the Association for Federal Information Resources Management, is also a superb monthly venue, and has always been a good place to meet agency IT managers. AFFIRM is a member council of ACT, the American Council for Technology (formerly the Federation of Government Information Processing Councils). ACT is a coalition of national and regional councils, including the Industry Advisory Council (IAC). If you sell information technology to the government, you have to understand the influence of the IAC. The events produced by ACT and its various member councils are important. The Western Information Technology Council (WITC) for instance, has the 16 Western states CIOs and regional Federal CIOs at an annual event.

There are also smaller special interest groups (SIGs) that are harder to spot. The PKI Working Group at the National Institutes of Standards and Technology (NIST) has representatives from many government agencies and industry working on public key infrastructure issues. Another NIST-based group is FISSEA – the Federal Information Systems Security Educators Association. Cyber security is deservedly hot, and FISSEA plays a significant role.

The list could go on for a long time and I know there are significant omissions, both good and bad.

My bottom line on major events is this: they cost lots of money, and without near-flawless execution, the return on investment is minimal, or worse, not measurable. The reality is there are

SIGs that might be better suited for your time and money, but research on your part is necessary to determine where the most influential players in your niche reside.

The major point of this whole diatribe is there are too many events. If for some reason you do not feel there are too many events, let me suggest you read any of the Federally-focused trade publications. Each produces events, and each also seems to be in league with others producing events. In itself, this is not bad, but it adds to the clutter and confusion. Many of the events produced by *Federal Computer Week* and *Government Computer News* target the same audience and even have the same speakers. Each also seems to have events at least monthly.

Similar to the theory of enough monkeys and enough typewriters, if you have enough money, enough people and enough time, you could attend all the events. Enough already.

If you are not yet confused by the clutter and confusion created by the event phenomena that will not go away, open your e-mail and see how many invitations you received while you were reading this.

Not that I have an opinion.

Appendix 8:

Glossary of Common Government Terms

Acquisition:

The acquiring of supplies or services by the federal government with appropriated funds through purchase or lease.

Affiliates:

Business concerns, organizations, or individuals that control each other or that are controlled by a third party. Control may include shared management or ownership; common use of facilities, equipment, and employees; or family interest.

Assignment of Claims:

This is done through ITSS when payment address needs to be changed to a financial institution. It is stored electronically and goes to finance for fund certification after CO makes changes. The two components of this are:

- Notice of Assignment

- Instrument of Assignment

Best and Final Offer (BAFO):

For negotiated procurements, a contractor's final offer following the conclusion of discussions.

Best Value:

The expected outcome of an acquisition that, in the Government's estimation, provides the greatest overall benefit in response to a requirement. A term applied to comparing proposals and ranking them from best to worst, not only on price but on all factors stated in the solicitation.

Business Information Centers (BICs):

One-stop locations for information, education, and training designed to help entrepreneurs start, operate, and grow their businesses. The centers provide free on-site counseling, training courses, and workshops and have resources for addressing a broad variety of business startup and development issues.

Certificate of Competency:

A certificate issued by the Small Business Administration (SBA) stating that the holder is "responsible" (in terms of capability, competency, capacity, credit, integrity, perseverance, and tenacity) for the purpose of receiving and performing a specific government contract.

Certified 8(a) Firm:

A firm owned and operated by socially and economically disadvantaged individuals and eligible to receive federal contracts under the Small Business Administration's 8(a) Business Development Program.

CFR:

Code of Federal Regulations

Contract:

A mutually binding legal relationship obligating the seller to furnish supplies or services (including construction) and the buyer to pay for them.

Contracting:

Purchasing, renting, leasing, or otherwise obtaining supplies or services from nonfederal sources. Contracting includes the description of supplies and services required, the selection and solicitation of sources, the preparation and award of contracts, and all phases of contract administration. It does not include grants or cooperative agreements.

Contracting Officer:

A person with the authority to enter into, administer, and/ or terminate contracts and make related determinations and findings.

Contractor Team Arrangement:

An arrangement in which (a) two or more companies form a partnership or joint venture to act as potential prime contractor; or (b) an agreement by a potential prime contractor with one or more other companies to have them act as its subcontractors under a specified government contract or acquisition program.

Defense Acquisition Regulatory Council (DARC):

A group composed of representatives from each military department, the Defense Logistics Agency, and the National Aeronautics and Space Administration, and that is in charge of the Federal Acquisition Regulation (FAR) on a joint basis with the Civilian Agency Acquisition Council (CAAC).

Defense Contractor:

Any person who enters into a contract with the United States for the production of material or for the performance of services for the national defense.

Determining the Extent of Competition:

Solicitation of three sources meets the requirement for maximum practicable competition for orders of $25,000 or less. Three is just a guideline. A list of sources should be maintained and continuously updated. The list should contain the status of each source (i.e., small business, veteran owned small business, small disadvantaged business, woman-owned small business) to ensure that small businesses are afforded opportunities to compete for simplified acquisitions. When using simplified acquisitions, maximum practical competition may be obtained without soliciting quotations or offers from sources outside the local trade area.

Direct Cite:*

Money does not go through the IT Fund. It is paid by the agency through DFAS. The vendor must go to DFAS to settle their account—it does not go through GSA. This money expires at the end of the fiscal year. Issued on a 1155 instead of GSA Form 300.

*Note: Not recommended to use unless IT Fund is low.

Electronic Data Interchange:

Transmission of information between computers using highly standardized electronic versions of common business documents.

Emerging Small Business:

A small business concern whose size is no greater than 50 percent of the numerical size standard applicable to the Standard Industrial Classification code assigned to a contracting opportunity.

Equity:

An accounting term used to describe the net investment of owners or stockholders in a business. Under the accounting equation, equity also represents the result of assets less liabilities.

Fair and Reasonable Price:

A price that is fair to both parties, considering the agreed-upon conditions, promised quality, and timeliness of contract performance. "Fair and reasonable" price is subject to statutory and regulatory limitations.

Federal Acquisition Regulation (FAR) :

The body of regulations which is the primary source of authority governing the government procurement process. The FAR, which is published as Chapter 1 of Title 48 of the Code of Federal Regulations, is prepared, issued, and maintained under the joint auspices of the Secretary of Defense, the Administrator of General Services Administration, and the Administrator of the National Aeronautics and Space Administration. Actual

responsibility for maintenance and revision of the FAR is vested
jointly in the Defense Acquisition Regulatory Council (DARC)
and the Civilian Agency Acquisition Council (CAAC).

Full and Open Competition:

With respect to a contract action, "full and open" competition
means that all responsible sources are permitted to compete.

GSA:

General Services Administration, the agency responsible for
the Federal Supply Schedules and for buying and leasing office
space on behalf of the Executive branch.

Incremental Funding:

Used if the total task order is awarded and the dollar amount
of the work is more than the client has available as the desired
start time. Pricing for the project is totaled and assigned on the
contract, but the pricing is charged incrementally as it becomes
available. The overall scope of work and pricing does not
change from the original proposal. The incremental funds are
added by modifications, but the modifications are not supposed
to add on to the period of performance or to add money on to
the full amount of the contract.

Intermediary Organization:

Organizations that play a fundamental role in encouraging,
promoting, and facilitating business-to-business linkages and
mentor-protégé partnerships. These can include both nonprofit
and for-profit organizations: chambers of commerce; trade
associations; local, civic, and community groups; state and local
governments; academic institutions; and private corporations.

IT Fund:

A fund that is managed by the Government which agencies draw from to pay their costs. It is "no year money" meaning that it does not expire at the end of the fiscal year. It must be used to buy IT services and supplies.

Joint Venture:

In the SBA Mentor-Protégé Program, an agreement between a certified 8(a) firm and a mentor firm to perform a specific federal contract.

Justification & Analysis:

(over $100,000) Required for a sole source open market procurement that exceeds the simplified acquisition threshold. This J&A must have a statement from the client as to why the procurement is required to be sole source and a justification from GSA must accompany this in the official file.

(over $500,000) If a client requests a sole source or a particular brand name, they must indicate why and document it. An internal document is prepared and signed by the Contract Specialist, Contracting Officer, Contracts Program Director, and Competition Advocate. A routing slip, internal document that circulates through GSA for signatures, is used as a cover sheet for this document and the attachments are as follows (copies of):

- J&A
- Quote
- Funding document (MIPR)

Market Research:

Involves obtaining information specific to the item being purchased. The extent of market research will vary, depending on such factors as urgency, estimated dollar value, complexity of the requirement, and past experience. Some techniques for conducting market research may include any or all of the following:

- Contracting experts regarding capabilities to meet requirements

- Reviewing the results of recent market research undertaken to meet similar or identical requirements.

- Publishing formal requests for information in appropriate technical and scientific journals

- Querying government data bases that provide information relevant to agency acquisitions

- Participating in interactive, on-line communication among industry, acquisition personnel, and customers

- Obtaining source lists of similar items from other contracting activities or agencies, trade associations or other sources.

Mentor:

A business, usually large, or other organization that has created a specialized program to advance strategic relationships with small businesses.

MIPR *(Military Interagency Purchase Request)*:

A funding source document accessed through ITSS for all branches of the military. Be sure to make sure the amount on the MIPR is more or the same as the contracted amount.

Modification:

Authorized changes to a contract after contract award.

Types:

- Administrative Change: A unilateral contract change that does not affect the contractual rights of the parties, e.g., a change in the paying office.

- Change Order: A written order, signed by the CO, directing the contractor to make a change authorized by the "changes" clause. A change order is issued without the consent of the contractor.

- Supplemental Agreement: A contract modification that is accomplished by the mutual action of both parties.

Bilateral Modification:

A contract modification that is signed by the contractor and the CO. Used to make negotiated adjustments resulting from the issuance of a change order; definitive letter contracts; or reflect other agreements of the parties modifying the terms of contracts.

Unilateral Modification:

A contract modification that is signed only by the CO. Used to make administrative changes, issue change orders, or make changes authorized by other than a "changes" clause.

Negotiation:

Contracting through the use of either competitive or other-than-competitive proposals and discussions. Any contract awarded without using sealed bidding procedures is a negotiated contract.

North American Industry Classification System (NAICS):

The new term for the Standard Industrial Classification (SIC) system. It classifies establishments according to how they conduct their economic activity. Improved to accurately identify industries. Effective October 1, 2000. Can be found in the FAR 19.

NAICS code rundown:

- Look at dollar amounts and employee size for that NAICS Category.

- Supplies: Look at dollar amounts for an average for the last 3 years.

- Services/Manufacturing: Look at number of employees for the past 12 months.

One-Stop Capital Shops:

OSCSs are the SBA's contribution to the Empowerment Zones/ Enterprise Communities Program, an interagency initiative that provides resources to economically distressed communities. The shops provide a full range of SBA lending and technical assistance programs.

Other Direct Costs (*OD.C.'s*)/*Supplemental Resources:*

OD.C.'s are the costs of facilities, supplies and services provided by the contractor in support of task order performance, that would normally be provided by the government. The CSR shall determine that the proposed costs are necessary and the ACO, that the prices are fair and reasonable.

Orders:

- Delivery Order: work order against an existing contract for hardware/software.

- Task Order: work order against an existing contract for services.

Partnering:

A mutually beneficial business-to-business relationship based on trust and commitment and that enhances the capabilities of both parties.

Price Analysis:

To ensure "fair and reasonable" prices. The FAR addresses two methods of analysis: 1) Price and 2) cost. Price analysis is the more appropriate method when using simplified acquisition procedures because it's less complex, less time-consuming, and less expensive.

Techniques:

- Competing offers
- Established catalog prices/market prices
- Price set by law or policy/regulations
- Previous contracts
- Previous quotes
- Prices of similar items
- Government estimates
- Visual analysis
- Value analysis

Price Negotiation Memorandum:

This document is used if GSA enters negotiations and indicates the prices are fair and reasonable. Done with all 8(a)'s over $100,000.

Prime Contract:

A contract awarded directly by the Federal government.

Procurement Plan:

Completed for 8(a) businesses and provides an outline of actions for the contract. An internal document. Contract

Specialist and a Contracting Officer sign-off on.

Protégé:

A firm in a developmental stage that aspires to increase its capabilities through a mutually beneficial business-to-business relationship.

Purchase Order:

Should include:

- Specific date for delivery of supplies or performance of services

- Appropriate clauses

- Trade and prompt payment discounts

- Quantity of items or scope of services

- Provisions for inspection & acceptance at destination
  ---If an offer is by the Government to supplier to buy certain supplies or services under specified terms or conditions:

- Issued on fixed-price basis and can't be open market in excess of $100,000

PO becomes a contract when:

- Acceptance of the order in writing is obtained at the outset by the contractor

- The contractor proceeds with the work to the point of substantial performance

- The contractor furnishes the supplies or services

Request for Proposal (RFP):

A document outlining a government agency's requirements and the criteria for the evaluation of offers.

SCORE:

The Service Corps of Retired Executives (SCORE) is a 12,400-member volunteer association sponsored by the SBA. SCORE matches volunteer business-management counselors with present prospective small business owners in need of expert advice.

SES:

Senior Executive Service

SEWP Contracts:

NASA contracts which have been pre-competed so no additional competition is required. NASA charges a .75% access fee.

Small Business:

A business smaller than a given size as measured by its employment, business receipts, or business assets.

Small Business Criteria:

- Entire business entity is considered (including parent company)

- The business does not dominate the fields it operates in.

- Must be organized for profit.

- Must be listed within the SBA to know NAICS (SIC) code standards that apply to them.

- Must meet employee and income requirements to meet small business classification (NAICS codes)

Socially Disadvantaged Business:

- Must meet NAICS (SIC) code standards—size and income

- More than 50% ownership must be: 1) African Americans; 2) Hispanic Americans; 3) Native Americans

- Day to day operations must be run by a person in one of these groups

- Not considered a set aside

Small Business Development Centers (SBDC):

SBDCs offer a broad spectrum of business information and guidance as well as assistance in preparing loan applications.

Small Business Innovative Research (SBIR) Contract:

A type of contract designed to foster technological innovation by small businesses with 500 or fewer employees. The SBIR contract program provides for a three-phased approach to research and development projects: technological feasibility and concept development, the primary research effort, and the conversion of the technology to a commercial application.

193

Small Disadvantaged Business Concern:

A small business concern that is at least 51 percent owned by one or more individuals who are both socially and economically disadvantaged. This can include a publicly owned business that has at least 51 percent of its stock unconditionally owned by one or more socially and economically disadvantaged individuals and whose management and daily business is controlled by one or more such individuals.

Spot Reductions:

A small reduction from your regular GSA Schedule price for a specific agency, usually a one-time event.

Standard Industrial Classification (SIC) Code:

A code representing a category within the Standard Industrial Classification System administered by the Statistical Policy Division of the U.S. Office of Management and Budget. The system was established to classify all industries in the U.S. economy. A two-digit code designates each major industry group, which is coupled with a second two-digit code representing subcategories.

Subcontract:

A contract between a prime contractor and a subcontractor to furnish supplies or services for the performance of a prime contract or subcontract.

Woman-Owned Small Business:

- Must meet NAICS codes

- More than 50% ownership must be women

- Day to day operations must be run by a woman